LANGUAGE AND LANGUAGE LEARNING

General Editors: RONALD MACKIN *and* PETER STREVENS

Usus quem penes arbitrium est et jus et norma loquendi.
(Usage, in whose hands lies the judgement, the law,
and the rule of speech.)

HORACE: *Ars Poetica*

Ye knowe ek, that in forme of speche is chaunge
Withinne a thousand yeer, and wordes tho
That hadden pris, now wonder nice and straunge
Us thinketh hem; and yit they spake hem so,
And spedde as wel in love as men now do.

CHAUCER

Language is an instrument that must as occasion re-
quires be bent to one's purpose. To stick to language as
it is can only lead to a sort of Philistinism which insists
on the observance of the cliché and will end up with a
hara-kiri of living thought. Indeed, the guardian of
language who jealously watches over its 'correctness'
is in the long run bound to turn into a reactionary who
looks askance at any innovation. Correctness is a useful,
but a negative virtue. Follow those prophets, and you
will soon find yourself imprisoned in a language cage,
clean, disinfected, and unpleasant like a sanatorium
room.

F. WAISMANN, 1962

Attitudes to English Usage

An Enquiry by the
University of Newcastle upon Tyne
Institute of Education English Research Group

W. H. MITTINS
MARY SALU
MARY EDMINSON
SHEILA COYNE

London

OXFORD UNIVERSITY PRESS

1970

Oxford University Press, Ely House, London W.1

GLASGOW NEW YORK TORONTO MELBOURNE WELLINGTON
CAPE TOWN SALISBURY IBADAN NAIROBI DAR ES SALAAM LUSAKA ADDIS ABABA
BOMBAY CALCUTTA MADRAS KARACHI LAHORE DACCA
KUALA LUMPUR SINGAPORE HONG KONG TOKYO

SBN 19 437041 0

PRINTED IN GREAT BRITAIN BY HEADLEY BROTHERS LTD
109 KINGSWAY LONDON WC2 AND ASHFORD KENT

Contents

ITEMS DISCUSSED SEPARATELY:

1

The purpose of the enquiry

The territory of English-teaching has long been something of a battle-field. Among the many issues now being fought out is that between 'prescriptive' and 'descriptive' attitudes to usage. The prescriptive, normative, authoritarian attitude is supported by a long tradition of 'rules', a tradition especially strong since the eighteenth century. Within this tradition, grammarians have shown considerable ingenuity in finding reasons for insisting on their preferred usages. Various criteria have been invoked to suit varying linguistic circumstances. One of the commonest appeals has been to the Latin model, as—for instance—when Landor dismissed '*under* the circumstances' as improper on the ground that one can't be under what is around (Latin 'circum'). A different etymology is still sometimes adduced in the attempt—as vain as such things invariably are—to limit the reference of *between* to two items, on the strength of derivation from *bi-twain*. Another criterion—that of grammatical accuracy—is still sometimes said to require '*much* pleased' instead of '*very* pleased' or, by association with Latin, '*their* (not *them*) being found out'. Different again is the insistence on 'go slow*ly*' rather than 'go slow', where the force of analogy allows the frequency of adverbs in -*ly* (from Old English -*lic*) to cast doubt on an equally legitimate alternative derived from an O.E. form in -*e*. It is usually logic that is called in to condemn 'try *and* come' and the dangling participle. On the other hand, meaning—'essential' meaning—is said to require '*becoming* angry', not '*getting* angry'. The character of these various authorities is often questionable and no more conclusive than the myths and linguistic folklore that generate what Fitzedward Hall called 'ipsedixitisms'.[1] In the 1870s, for example, the 'rule' that demanded '*down* to this time' instead of '*up* to this time' asserted with a grand arbitrariness that time was reckoned *up* to the dawn of history but *down* thereafter.[2]

At the opposite extreme to traditional prescriptive forces stands the

---

[1] From Latin 'ipse dixit' = 'he himself said it'. Hence, a dogmatic assertion unsupported by evidence or reasoning.

[2] Letter in *Notes and Queries*, 5th Series, Vol. VII, 1877, p. 137.

objective descriptive approach characteristic of modern linguistic science. For the modern 'linguistician' (or modern 'linguist', as we shall hereafter call him, since no question of mastery of foreign languages is involved in our enquiry) 'correctness' of usage is a misleading notion that should give way to concepts of acceptability and appropriateness. Even if 'correct' were deemed in the social situation to be more or less equivalent to 'acceptable' (in the same sense as 'correct' dress and 'correct' table-manners), from a purely linguistic angle the two notions need to be dissociated. American linguists have often given the distinction a sharp edge. Thus C. C. Fries (1940) asserts that 'there can never be in grammar an error that is both very bad and very common'; and R. A. Hall (1964) contends that 'the only time we can call any usage totally incorrect is when it would never be used by any native speaker of the language, no matter what his social or intellectual standing'. In an earlier book (1960), Hall in fact claimed to be looking forward to a time, doubtless far distant, when 'a claim to dispensing "correct" speech will be treated as being equal in fraudulence to a claim to dispensing a cure-all in medicine'.

One must not, of course, assume unquestioningly that authority necessarily resides with the modern linguists any more than with the traditional supporters of 'correctness'. There are those, indeed, who argue quite the reverse. The American Follett (1966), for example, sees the opposition as between, on the one hand, a large and sensible majority that includes 'everybody from the proverbial plain man to the professional writer', and on the other hand 'an embattled minority, who make up for their small number by their great learning and their place of authority in the school system and the world of scholarship'. The former, in Follett's view very properly, take it for granted that 'there is a right way to use words and construct sentences, and many wrong ways. The right way is believed to be clearer, more logical, and hence more likely to prevent error and confusion.' Contrariwise, the latter 'deny that there is such a thing as correctness . . . their governing principle is epitomized in the title of a speech by a distinguished member of the profession: "Can Native Speakers of a Language Make Mistakes?".' If there were any doubt which side Follett is on, it would be dispelled by his demand for 'the increasingly obvious and imperative reform—a resumption in our schools of the teaching of grammar and the reading of books'. (This final requirement is perhaps more relevant to the American than to the British scene, but in any case is not strictly pertinent to this enquiry.)

The work of teachers of English, and, incidentally, of teachers in general, involves them in the issues raised by the prescriptive/descriptive opposition. In practice, if not necessarily in theory, they must adopt some sort of attitude to usage. It seems unlikely that many would take a completely descriptive line; even if they tried to do so they would probably still exercise indirect and unintentional influence. Nor does total prescriptivism seem a reasonably tenable or realistic position for a teacher—or indeed anybody else—in a conspicuously permissive age. How, then, may teachers find a middle position that avoids on the one hand seeming abdication of responsibility ('anything goes'), on the other hand Canute-like insistence on linguistic practices not endorsed by contemporary society or even by colleagues? One obvious prerequisite for reasonable choice of stance is information about current usage and attitudes to usage.

Our main purpose was to add to the stock of such information. The immediate objective was an assessment of how acceptable a number of specific disputed usages were. To this end, we sought a sample of reactions to usages of this kind. Our sample allowed for a number of variables. The items themselves varied in verbal mode, i.e. speech or writing; the situations in which they were to be thought of varied in 'tone', i.e. formal or informal; and the respondents varied in age, occupation, and—within the 'educationist' category—in role (student, teacher, examiner, etc.).

Information from such a sampling is, in itself, of limited value, especially in the eyes of those who maintain that 'debatable' usages constitute a very small fraction of total language. We hoped, however, to infer from the particular results a notion of the general character and distribution of views on acceptability of usage. We were also interested in setting current attitudes and judgements in a historical context: to what extent, we wondered, were teachers and other educated adults sustaining a pre-scientific tradition? And in addition we wanted to satisfy our curiosity about an interesting area of linguistic behaviour.

2

The form of the enquiry

No attempt was made to systematize the selection of particular usages. Most of the items chosen seemed to us to be currently subject to variation in practice and dispute in theory. A few others were included because, if not obviously contentious today, they had been sufficiently so in the past to have been used in earlier enquiries of this kind. One or two were of special interest to one or other of us.

Respondents were invited, not to record their own linguistic practice, but to estimate the favourableness or otherwise of their spontaneous reaction to each usage when encountered in four types of situation— Informal Speech, Informal Writing, Formal Speech, Formal Writing. To the main fifty items were added five which it was assumed—over-hastily, as it proved—would not occur naturally in all four situations. We still feel justified in having restricted *onto* (No. 51) and *alright* (No. 54) to written contexts, since the alternative single-word and two-word forms are usually indistinguishable in speech, but the assumption that '*Who* was he looking for?' (No. 52) and 'Between you and *I*' (No. 55) were unthinkable in Formal Writing, now looks rash. (Our temerity was very properly corrected, at least for No. 52, by the distinguished linguist who insisted that he normally used and therefore accepted the 'Who . . . for?' pattern in the most formal circumstances.) The fifth item—'Go *slow*' (No. 53)—was even more unreasonably excluded by us from both formal situations (spoken and written), on the insufficient ground that the tone of the whole utterance (That's a dangerous curve; you'd better go slow) was clearly informal.

While realizing that a certain degree of arbitrariness was unavoidable, we spent some time considering how to maximize consensus in the interpretation of the four-situation framework. At one time it seemed that detailed exposition with examples might obviate demarcation disputes, but we concluded that it was impossible satisfactorily to define the four areas without overloading the prolegomena and inviting more argument than would be disposed of. Accordingly we limited the briefing to a note offering something like a standard orientation towards the exercise without—we hoped—attracting undue attention to its arbitrary features. This explanatory note read:

A debatable usage is one accepted by some people and not by others. Our object is to discover the nature and extent of agreement and of disagreement over certain usages of this kind in English.

We are interested in varying attitudes to these usages in different situations. We are not seeking opinions on what is 'right' or 'wrong', nor are we asking about your own practice in speech or writing.

Disregarding notions of 'correctness', then, please imagine that you hear or read each item in the situations indicated. Record your immediate reaction to the *underlined*[1] part as either acceptance or the contrary by making a tick or a cross in the appropriate place. If you find it quite impossible to decide, put a question mark. Items 51–55 are rather different in that not all four kinds of situation are likely to occur; some of the spaces are accordingly blocked out.

The following quotation from the *English Journal* (Champaign, Illinois, February 1962) suggests what we are trying to do:

'Can an English teacher really maintain his position as a language policeman? The language has gone on "degenerating", all his million admonitions notwithstanding. In our secret heart we must all know that certain usages will come into prominence and others drop out, and there is absolutely nothing we can do about it. About all we can do for those easily intimidated by social shibboleths is to locate all the objective data available and say "In this area among these people at this time . . . . is currently in vogue".'

The covering letter to respondents also included a request for personal particulars (mainly occupation and age) and an invitation to suggest further debatable items, with comment on them and any other relevant matter. These documents were sent out (or, in the case of students, delivered by hand) to over 500 people of various occupations. The 457 answers came from:

57 school teachers of English

35 external examiners of school English (e.g. General Certificate of Education (G.C.E.), Royal Society of Arts (R.S.A.))

---

[1] Italics have replaced the underlining used in the actual questionnaire. Particular words under discussion have also been italicized in some quotations.

30	school teachers of subjects other than English
37	university teachers
22	lecturers in colleges of education
41	lecturers in commercial and technical colleges
79	teacher-trainees in a university department of education
46	mature teacher-trainees in a college of education
50	teacher-trainees in a 'general' college of education
22	managerial staff in commerce and industry
5	salesmen, advertisers, or public relations officers
9	professional writers
11	administrators (e.g. Civil Service, National Coal Board, local government)
13	doctors, clergymen, solicitors, barristers

457

Respondents belonging to more than one of these categories were assigned to the more restricted or specialized of their occupations. Thus, one or two dons with considerable reputations as novelists were counted as professional writers, and teacher-examiners were treated as examiners.

The actual questionnaire was as follows:

	Informal		*Formal*	
	Speech	*Writing*	*Speech*	*Writing*
1. He did not do *as* well as the experts had expected.				
2. The audience was *very* amused.				
3. The conservative-minded are averse *to* making any changes.				
4. Traditional and *contemporary* furniture do not go well together.				
5. The data *is* sufficient for our purpose.				
6. The members of the team laughed at *each other*.				

	Informal		Formal	
	Speech	Writing	Speech	Writing
7. We *have got* to finish the job.				
8. Young girls do not dress *the way* their grandmothers did.				
9. *Under* these circumstances no-one should complain.				
10. He is in London, but his family *are* in Bournemouth.				
11. The agreement *between* the four powers was cancelled.				
12. Answer *either* Question 1 *or* Question 2 *or* both.				
13. It was not *all that* easy.				
14. They will send the poultry *providing* the tax is low.				
15. The performance ended early, *due to* illness among the players.				
16. We *met up with* him at the Zoo.				
17. The instruments were *pretty* reliable.				
18. There were *less* road accidents this Christmas than last.				
19. Competitors should try *and* arrive in good time.				
20. The process is *very unique*.				
21. He is older than *me*.				

	Informal		Formal	
	Speech	Writing	Speech	Writing
22. They work *evenings* and *Sundays*.				
23. They behaved differently at school *than* they did at home.				
24. He *only had* one chapter to finish.				
25. His eyes were *literally* standing out of his head.				
26. They invited my friends and *myself*.				
27. What are the chances of *them* being found out?				
28. Intoxication is *when* the brain is affected by certain stimulants.				
29. Their success, his attitude *inferred*, was due to his own efforts.				
30. He refused *to even think* of it.				
31. They would accept this if it *was* offered.				
32. He did it *quicker* than he had ever done it before.				
33. He did not actually dislike football; he was just *disinterested*.				
34. Reference will be made to the *historic* development of mathematics.				
35. Neither author nor publisher *are* subject to censorship.				

	Informal		Formal	
	Speech	Writing	Speech	Writing
36. One rarely likes to do as *he* is told.				
37. Roller-skating is very different *to* ice-skating.				
38. *These sort of plays* need first-class acting.				
39. You will learn that *at university.*				
40. *Pulling the trigger*, the gun went off unexpectedly.				
41. He could write *as well or better than* most people.				
42. She told Charles and *I* the whole story.				
43. It was *us* who had been singing.				
44. Nowadays Sunday is not observed *like* it used to be.				
45. He told me the story and I *implied* a great deal from it.				
46. They bought some tomatoes *off* a barrow-boy.				
47. It looked *like* it would rain.				
48. I *will* be twenty-one tomorrow.				
49. Everyone has *their* off-days.				
50. They will *loan* you the glasses.				
51. He jumped *onto* the roof of the shed.				

	Informal		Formal	
	Speech	*Writing*	*Speech*	*Writing*
52. *Who* was he looking for?				▨
53. That's a dangerous curve; you'd better go *slow*.			▨	▨
54. In spite of the delay, everything was *alright*.	▨		▨	
55. Between you and *I*, she drinks heavily.				▨

(Readers who were not consulted might find it interesting, before reading further, to note their own responses.)

3

Survey of responses

A. Items 1–50
With 457 respondents considering 50 items, each in four types of
situation, the number of judgements totalled $457 \times 50 \times 4 = 91,400$.

The request not to resort to Doubtful (?) except when it was quite
impossible to decide between Accept (✓) and Reject (X) was so
readily acceded to that hardly more than 1 per cent of the responses
were indeterminate.

The following table indicates the pattern of responses both in the
four separate situations and compositely:

Table 1

	Total No.	%	Informal Speech No.	%	Informal Writing No.	%	Formal Speech No.	%	Formal Writing No.	%
Accept (✓)	36,997	41	13,970	61	10,575	46	7,046	31	5,406	24
Reject (X)	53,183	58	8,611	38	11,989	53	15,487	68	17,096	75
Doubtful (?)	1,220	1	269	1	286	1	317	1	348	1
TOTAL	91,400	100	22,850	100	22,850	100	22,850	100	22,850	100

The table shows a general tendency, of the order of nearly 3 to 2
(58 to 41 per cent), towards rejection rather than acceptance. Only in
the least stringent of the four settings—Informal Speech—was there a
majority (61 per cent) of acceptances. Elsewhere, permissiveness fell
from nearly half (46 per cent) in Informal Writing to under a third (31
per cent) in Formal Speech and less than a quarter (24 per cent) in
Formal Writing. It is doubtful, of course, how much reliance can be placed
on judgements made in experimental conditions. Some respondents,
perhaps those most familiar with modern linguistics and its advocacy of
descriptive as against prescriptive attitudes to usage, may unconsciously
have represented themselves as *more* tolerant than they really are.
But such cases would probably be easily outnumbered by those who,

consciously or unconsciously, were 'put on their mettle' by the test situation and expressed *less* tolerant reactions than their ordinary language behaviour warranted.

The predominance of censoriousness over permissiveness was reflected in correspondents' suggestions of additional items of debatable usage. The invitation to extend the list of debatable usages produced well over two hundred different new items, of which the great majority were explicitly or implicitly condemned. There were one or two pleas for tolerance (e.g. 'of such local habits of speech as "To get a hold of" ') and a few expressions of genuine uncertainty (e.g. five foot/feet high). But (incidentally, the initial use of *but* or *and* was included on the black list!) by far the commonest sentiments expressed were those of disapproval, irritation, shock and guilt. Alleged mis-usages were attributed to laziness, slovenliness, lack of discrimination, meaninglessness, confusion, inaccuracy, deterioration, degeneration and contamination. The offending items included traditional textbook 'errors' (e.g. *quite* a few), colloquialisms (especially *aggravate* for *annoy*), dialect (e.g. it is not his *blame*), and Americanisms actual (e.g. *stop off at*) and putative (e.g. *blown-up* for *enlarged*). Nearly always (another censored usage!) it was possible to infer the choice involved—however unrealistic or outdated or pedantic it might seem to some people—but a few usages seemed not only unobjectionable but irreplaceable. What, for instance, is the preferred alternative to *a modified version*, *as soon as possible*, or indeed *nearly always*? The 'witch-hunting' attitude which seems to develop so rapidly in the field of usage was perhaps well illustrated by the respondent who took us to task for using the plural verb in the instruction 'Please tick whichever of the following descriptions *fit* you'. Presumably in his zeal he overlooked the possibility that an individual might belong to more than one occupational category—teacher *and* examiner, professional writer *and* lecturer/doctor, etc. Or perhaps he would insist that 'whichever' can have only singular reference and that we should have said something like 'Tick such of the following descriptions as fit you'.

The presentation of the four 'situations' in the order Informal Speech through Informal Writing and Formal Speech to Formal Writing may have encouraged respondents to express their decline in toleration in that same sequence. But the very marked infrequency of departures from the left-to-right order suggests that at most the mode of presentation reinforced an already strong tendency. Though in general speech allows of more freedom in usage than writing, the mode of communication is clearly felt to be subsidiary to the level of formality existing between the communicators.

By averaging the four situation-responses to each of the main fifty items it was possible to establish a percentage acceptance-rate for each. On this basis, the order of general acceptability was:

Table 2

The Main Fifty Items in Order of General Acceptability

Order	% Acceptance	Item No.	Usage
1	86	1	did not do *as* well as
2	81	3	averse *to*
3	76	2	*very* amused
4	70	4	*contemporary* (= modern) furniture
5	69	5	data *is*
6	67	39	*at university*
7	64	9	*Under* these circumstances
8	59	6	laughed at *each other* (more than two)
9	57	11	*between* the four powers
10	57	12	*either ... or ... or*
11	56	48	I *will* be twenty-one tomorrow
12	50	7	We *have got* to finish
13	47	14	They will send ... *providing* the tax is low
14	47	10	his family *are*
15	46	31	if it *was* offered
16	46	22	They work *evenings* and *Sundays*
17	45	24	He *only had* one chapter to finish
18	45	8	do not dress *the way* their grandmothers did
19	43	15	ended early, *due to* illness
20	42	49	Everyone has *their* off-days
21	42	21	He is older than *me*
22	42	32	He did it *quicker*
23	40	27	the chances of *them* being found out
24	40	30	*to even think* of it
25	39	17	were *pretty* reliable
26	38	41	*as well or better than* most
27	38	13	not *all that* easy
28	37	28	Intoxication is *when*
29	37	29	his attitude *inferred* (for 'implied')
30	35	18	*less* road accidents
31	35	25	eyes were *literally* standing out of his head
32	34	33	he was just *disinterested* (for 'uninterested')
33	33	26	invited my friends and *myself*
34	31	35	neither author nor publisher *are*
35	30	37	is very different *to*
36	30	23	behaved differently ... *than*
37	29	38	*These sort of plays* need
38	29	34	the *historic* development of mathematics
39	27	19	should try *and* arrive
40	27	42	told Charles and *I*
41	25	43	It was *us* who

(*continued on next page*)

Table 2 (*continued*)

Order	% Acceptance	Item No.	Usage
42	24	44	is not observed *like* it used to be
43	22	50	They will *loan* you the glasses
44	20	36	One rarely likes to do as *he* is told
45	19	46	bought some tomatoes *off* a barrow-boy
46	17	40	*Pulling the trigger,* the gun went off
47	14	16	We *met up with* him
48	12	47	It looked *like* it would rain
49	12	45	I *implied* (for 'inferred') a great deal from it
50	11	20	*very unique*

No one aware of the complex of factors that seems to influence views on linguistic respectability would venture to make any firm inferences from this order. In few human operations can such a mixture of tradition, prejudice, myth and irrelevance be found. In any case, it would be unwise to generalize from an order of acceptability based on average ratings derived from four sets of judgements.

It is none the less tempting to pose a few questions as matter for speculation. Does Table 2 reflect, for instance, a special harshness towards what are believed to be Americanisms (*met up with* is 47th and the construction '*one . . . he*' 44th out of 50)? Are some of the most acceptable usages no longer debatable for many people? Were some of the younger respondents even aware of the traditional if obsolescent insistence on 'not *so* well as' (Item 1) or '*much* amused' (Item 2)? Does the decline in the study of the classics largely account for the comparatively favourable reception of 'averse *to*' rather than '*from*' (2nd), '*under* (for *in*) these circumstances' (7th) and 'data *is*' (5th)? Is it mainly a sense of logic—perhaps exaggerated—that places '*very* unique' (50th) and the 'dangling' participle (46th) at the bottom of the list?

Another line of speculation that raises interesting, though probably unanswerable, questions about some of the items concerns whether an item may have been judged as an isolated phenomenon, or in relation to usages elsewhere on the list, or as a sample of a whole class of disputed usages. One wonders, for instance, whether the low ranking (41st) of 'It was *us* who . . .' would have been shared by the analogous but more familiar 'It is *me*', 'It's *me*', 'It was *them*'. Would not 'come *and* see' have been received much more favourably than the similar (and equally unobjectionable?) 'try *and* arrive' (39th)? Why should the blurring of the infer/imply distinction seem so much more objectionable when 'implied' replaces traditional 'inferred' (49th) than when the reverse happens (29th)? Obviously, a fuller and more delicate investigation would be needed to establish anything like reliable answers to these questions.

Are certain kinds of disputed items less acceptable than other kinds? Any classification by kind must necessarily be crude and arbitrary, but a rough-and-ready division might be made under five headings, according to the assumed dominant factor on which opinion diverges:

(a) Colloquial items, usually associated with informal speech: e.g. not *all that* easy, *pretty* reliable.

(b) Etymological items, where the censorious critic normally appeals to derivation (especially Latin roots): e.g. data *is*, different *to*.

(c) Grammatical items, of various kinds, where alleged misuse concerns concord (*these sort of plays*), case (told Charles and *I*), proximity (he *only had*), choice of part of speech (did it *quicker*), etc.

(d) Lexical/semantic items where the offence is thought to involve a distortion of meaning: e.g. the confusion of inferred/implied, historic/historical, disinterested/uninterested.

(e) Language myths, where the censorious tend to invoke a prescription of dubious authority: e.g. not *as* well as, *due to*, or the dangling participle.

Clearly some items can claim to be considered under more than one of these headings. For the sake of getting some sort of impression, one might, however—with considerable arbitrariness—assign each item as follows:

(a) Colloquial items: 7 8 13 16 17 22 39 46
(b) Etymological items: 3 5 9 23 37
(c) Grammatical items: 6 10 11 12 21 24 30 32 35 36 38 41 42 43 44 47 49 50
(d) Lexical/semantic items: 2 4 18 19 20 25 28 29 33 34 45 48
(e) Language myths: 1 14 15 26 27 31 40

Only to the limited extent that this classification is acceptable as a working assumption may significance be attached to the order of acceptability of these five sets:

Table 3

Order	Set	% Acceptability	No. of items
1	(b) Etymological	55	5
2	(e) Myths	45	7
3	(a) Colloquial	40	8
4	(d) Lexical/semantic	38	12
5	(c) Grammatical	37	18

No such categorization was envisaged when the test was designed and no particular importance should be attached to the exact correspondence between the order of acceptability of the sets (from more to less acceptable) and the order of size (from smaller to larger). Presumably the panel tended to favour lexical and grammatical items (in the sense applied in the above classification) because such items occupy a large part of the debatable area. In any case, the difference in acceptability between the last three sets (40 – 37 per cent) is too small to be significant. But the comparative acceptability of the 'myths', and still more conspicuously of the etymological items, is worth notice. A possible factor has already been mentioned—the decline in classical studies, with a consequently diminished sense of derivation (e.g. of 'data' as plural, or of 'under' as incompatible with '*circum*stances') and of Latin-oriented 'rules' (e.g. subjunctive after 'if', possessive before -ing verb).

These tentative observations are made on the strength of acceptability ratings which are themselves derived by averaging responses in the four different situations. Such averaging eliminates the factor of 'spread' that is, the extent of the variation in responses between the extremes of Informal Speech and Formal Writing. (Whereas, for example, '*pretty* reliable' was found acceptable in Informal Speech by 84 per cent of judges but in Formal Writing only by 7 per cent, the corresponding 'spread' of 'I *implied* a great deal from it' was only from 16 to 8 per cent.) It would be very laborious and—in view of the arbitrary nature of the classification—not very profitable to work out acceptability orders for the five sets of items in terms of the four separate situations. It can be assumed, however, that colloquialisms would occupy a high position (almost certainly the top rank) in the Informal Speech table and a correspondingly low position in the Formal Writing table. This assumption is justified by the order of the five sets in regard to extent of 'spread'. This order, from greatest to least 'spread', is:

> Colloquialisms
> Grammatical Items
> Myths
> Lexical/semantic items
> Etymological items.

Setting aside this classification, the particular items showing the greatest range of acceptability between Informal Speech and Formal Writing, in order of this 'spread', were:

Order by Spread		Item	Acceptability-rating (out of 50)
1	17	*pretty* reliable	25
2	7	*have got* to	12
3	13	not *all that* easy	27
4	21	older than *me*	21
5	24	*only had* one	24

These are all very common colloquial or conversational usages of marked lexical simplicity. By contrast, the items showing the least 'spread' of response between the two extreme situations have a distinctly technical flavour; four of them involve comparatively advanced vocabulary, and the fifth—the dangling participle—a sophisticated sense of grammatical structure. These five items are:

Order by Spread		Item	Acceptability-rating (out of 50)
46	29	it *inferred*	29
47	40	*Pulling . . . ,* it	46
48	20	*very* unique	50
49	33	*dis*interested	32
50	45	I *implied*	49

The tendency for the top five items for 'spread' to occupy the middle ranges for general acceptability, whereas the bottom five mostly come from the least acceptable zone, warns us to remember that there is less scope for 'spread' among items at the ends of a scale than among those nearer the middle.

Respondents were asked to identify themselves on a list of 14 occupational categories. Most of them were able to classify themselves without difficulty, but—as anticipated—a few belonged to more than one category (combining, for instance, university teaching with professional writing). The only substantial overlap of this kind was between teachers of English (in schools and universities) and examiners in English for schools. These last were treated as examiners for the purpose of the enquiry. Otherwise, the heading under which an individual had first been thought of as a possible respondent was made the operative one.

Some of the groups were inevitably very small. The smallest comprised 5 salesmen or advertisers or public relations officers; the next, 9 professional writers. In the event categories were amalgamated to make five broad groups:

A   Teacher-trainee students in University Departments of
     Education (U.D.E.). and Colleges of Education   175
B   Teachers (of English and of other subjects)   87
C   Lecturers (in universities, colleges of education, commercial
     and technical colleges)   100
D   Examiners in English (mainly G.C.E.).   35
E   Non-educationists (industry, commerce, public relations,
     administration, professions other than education, writers)   60
                                                                    ———
                                                                     457
                                                                    ———

An estimate of the comparative tolerance of these five groups was
made by counting the percentages of rejections recorded in the two
extreme situations, Informal Speech and Formal Writing. These scores,
with two consolidations (of total teachers and of total educationists),
can be tabulated as follows:

Table 4

		Percentage Rejections		
		Informal Speech	*Formal Writing*	*Average*	*Order of Tolerance*
A	Students	30	68	49	I
B	Teachers	42	79	60½	4
C	Lecturers	42	78	60	3
D	Examiners	49	84	66½	5
E	Non-educationists	36	77	56½	2
A + B + C Total teachers		37	74	55½	
A + B + C + D Total educationists		38	75	56½	

The close correspondence between the figures for educationists as a
unitary group (A + B + C + D) and non-educationists (E) suggests
that, contrary to what is sometimes alleged, teachers and lecturers are
not excessively restrictive or pedantic about language matters. But
within the range of educationists, students seem much more and
examiners much less lenient than the others. The sharing of a high
rejection rate by non-educationists and educationists alike discourages
an interpretation that tolerance diminishes with increased involvement
in teaching and more particularly in examining. A more likely interpretation might stress the factor of age. If, as seems reasonable to assume,
examiners (because of the need for prior teaching experience) tend
to be on average older than teachers, the extreme positions of students

and examiners on the scale might be determined largely by the contrast between comparative youth and comparative age. (It was hoped to make a thorough analysis of all the replies by age-categories as well as occupation-groups, but time proved too short. However, a brief examination of responses by age-groups to a small sample of items—reported on pages 21 to 23 below—gives some indication of the weight of the age-factor.)

On the assumption that, whatever the determinants, the order of permissiveness by occupational groups (A–E–C–B–D) has some meaning, it is possible to note which items elicited responses most at variance from it. For this purpose, the pattern of group-response to each item can be worked out for the four 'situations' and their average. In this sense, a fully characteristic item would repeat the order A – E – C – B – D in each of the five cases.

Full agreement of this kind occurred with only two items: '*dis*interested' (Item 33) and 'told Charles and *I*' (Item 42). Only 'ties' under one heading excluded two others: 'historic' (Item 34) and 'different *to*' (Item 37). A further two—'literally' (Item 25) and '*them* being' (Item 27)—reflected the standard order in four of the five comparisons. Except for the last of these, which came 23rd in the general acceptability order, all were among the least acceptable usages (positions 31st to 40th out of 50).

Turning to items *un*characteristically treated by the occupational groups, it is possible to note a few quite sharp divergences. For example:

Students (Group A), though in general the most lenient group, were among the most critical of Items 1 (did not do *as* well as), 7 (*have got* to finish), 10 (family *are*) and 19 (try *and* arrive). Could it be that reaction to these items reflects the 'school-mastered' English that used to be, and presumably still is, taught in some schools?

Non-educationists (E, the next most tolerant group) were unusually harsh on three of these same items (1, 10, 19), and also on Items 30 (*to even think*), 31 (if it *was* offered) and 43 (It was *us* who).

Lecturers (Group C), being the middle group of the five, had little scope for wide variation.

School-teachers (Group B) were fairly consistently harsher than the average, but comparatively less so towards a handful of items that included Nos. 5 (the data *is*), 12 (*either . . . or . . . or*), 14 (*providing*, for 'provided'), 30 (*to even think*), 39 (*at university*), 43 (it was *us*) and 48 (I *will*, for 'shall').

Examiners (Group D) departed from their usual stringency to the extent of being more lenient than all other groups in their general reaction to Nos. 10 (family *are*), 17 (*pretty* reliable), 19 (try *and* arrive) and 31 (if it *was*). Teachers who argue that they have to prescribe usages they do not really believe in because they are sure examiners will not accept the alternatives might be interested to know that, in the Formal Writing category, examiners were the least lenient group for 31 of the 50 usages; for 11 usages, they were less harsh than one of the other groups; for 4 they occupied the middle position, 3rd of the 5 groups; for 3, they were more permissive than all but one group; and for 1 usage (Item 36, *One . . . he*) they were most permissive of all.

In general, this analysis reveals a variety of attitude even greater and more bewildering than was anticipated. The absence of any firm consensus of opinion is not to be regretted, since it springs from natural and inevitable causes (changes in language itself and variable responses to these changes). What is perhaps regrettable is that dogmatic and sometimes irrational or ignorant condemnation of change and innovation seemed to occur much more frequently than approval or acquiescence. Clearly the conceptions of 'good' as against 'bad' English and even of a single 'correct' language still exercise considerable influence, despite the doubts cast upon them by modern linguistic science.

B.   Items 51–55

Since each of these items was posed in only two or three of the four situations, with only one common denominator—Informal Writing—applicable in all five, straight comparisons either with other items or with each other are not feasible. No usable averages of general acceptability can be calculated. Nevertheless, it was quite clear that, of the five usages, '*Who* was he looking for?' (Item 52) was by any standard the most acceptable, and 'Between you and *I*' (Item 55) the least.

In the Informal Writing context, in which all were considered, the order of acceptability was:

Order		Item	% Acceptability
1	52.	*Who* was he looking for?	64
2	51.	He jumped *onto* the roof of the shed.	61
3	54.	In spite of the delay, everything was *alright*.	56
4	53.	That's a dangerous curve; you'd better go *slow*.	40
5	55.	Between you and *I*, she drinks heavily.	22

Items from the main fifty with similar acceptability percentages in Informal Writing were:

		% Acceptability	Order of Acceptability (out of 50)	
	Item	Informal Writing	Informal Writing	Total
7	We *have got* to finish the job	65	11	12
12	Answer *either . . . or . . . or . . .*	62	12	10
22	They work *evenings* and *Sundays*	56	14	16
18	There were *less* accidents this Christmas	39	30	30
36	*One* rarely likes to do as *he* is told	22	44	44

It is similarly impossible strictly to make comparisons in terms of occupational groups. The figures for the main items (Table 4, page 18) were drawn from responses in Informal Speech and Formal Writing, whereas—as we have noted—the only possible calculations for Items 51–55 must be based on Informal Writing. These last figures, as expected, fall between the two sets (Informal Speech, Formal Writing) of the main group. Nevertheless, they may be of some interest:

Table 5 (Items 51–55)

		% Rejections in Informal Writing	Order of Permissiveness
A	Students	22	1
B	Teachers	39	2
C	Lecturers	48	4
D	Examiners	51	5
E	Non-educationists	43	3
A + B + C	Total teachers	33	
A + B + C + D	Total educationists	35	

As with the main fifty items, the most tolerant group is of students (A), the least tolerant examiners (D). The other three groups fall into a different order from that in the main enquiry, but this difference is rendered insignificant by the fairly narrow band of percentages involved for Items 51–55 (39–48 per cent) and the even narrower band for Items 1–50 (on average, $56\frac{1}{2}$–$60\frac{1}{2}$ per cent). Nor is it possible to attach any importance to the wider gap (for Items 51–55) between the rates of educationists as a whole (35 per cent) and non-educationists (43 per cent).

C. A Note about Age

As mentioned above (page 19), shortage of time forced us to abandon our intention of making a second complete analysis of our data by age-categories. But a limited examination of responses to a sample of eleven of the items confirmed the expectation that tolerance tends to vary inversely with age.

Of the 457 judges, the 443 who indicated which of six age-groups they belonged to were distributed as follows:

Table 6

Numbers in Age-Groups

Group	Under 25	25–30	31–40	41–50	51–65	Over 65	Total
A	112	22	24	8			166
B	14	6	24	22	20		86
C	1	9	32	30	28		100
D	1	1	9	8	14	2	35
E	2	3	13	21	15	2	56
	130	41	102	89	77	4	443
= %	29	9	23	20	18	1	100

Group A   were students training to teach, in a U.D.E. or College of Education; one of the two colleges was for 'mature' students only.

Group B   were teachers (not only of English).

Group C   were lecturers, in universities and various kinds of colleges.

Group D   were examiners, mainly for G.C.E.

Group E   were professional men and women not primarily employed in the education service; they included industrialists, businessmen, administrators, writers, etc.

The degree of acceptance by these age-groups of the eleven items can be tabulated:

Table 7

Percentage of Various Age-Groups Accepting Sample Items

Nos. in Age-Groups:	130	41	102	89	77	4	443
Age:	Under 25	25–30	31–40	41–50	51–65	Over 65	Total
Item No.	%	%	%	%	%	%	%
7	51	46	50	50	50	49	50
9	74	73	62	58	49	50	63
15	56	51	37	34	34	63	43
17	42	37	43	37	40	25	40
18	50	41	29	28	23	38	35
21	47	38	48	38	31	50	42
24	58	49	42	30	35	64	44
25	55	40	26	22	22	25	34
27	49	49	40	29	29	38	39
28	49	39	35	28	31	25	37
31	52	54	42	38	47	50	46
All 11 items	53	47	41	36	35	43	43

Notes: (a) The percentages are calculated from the averages of the four situation-responses of each individual.

(b) The slight difference (1 per cent) between the total acceptance-percentage for some of the items and the corresponding figures in Table 2 above (pages 13 to 14) is due to the different total numbers of responses used, as not all judges revealed their ages.

(c) The total acceptance rate for the eleven items (43 per cent) is slightly higher (by 2 per cent) than the total for all items (41 per cent) as shown in Table 1 (page 11).

The over-65 figures, obtained from only four respondents, are, of course, not significant. But the pattern below that age shows a well-defined decline in tolerance from the under-25s to the 50-plus group. It seems unlikely that this decline is due *solely* to a tendency for the individual to become more censorious (respectable?) with advancing years, or *solely* to the alleged general growth in the twentieth century of laxity (liberalness?). The relative contribution of these two factors, and of any others that may contribute, is a matter to be left to speculation.

4

Discussion of separate items

ITEM 1.   He did not do *as* well as the experts had expected.

A long tradition has favoured '*so* . . . as' after the negative *not*, rather than the 'positive' construction '*as* . . . as'. The *Oxford English Dictionary*, remarking that *so* is used especially in negative sentences, cites examples from as early as 1366. But, as often, the practice of distinguished writers has defied theory; Marckwardt and Walcott (1938) note that Storm (in *Englische Philologie*) found 'not . . . *as* . . . as' in Swift, Johnson, Boswell, Dickens, Marryat, Trollope and others.

The old 'rule' has survived into the twentieth century, on both sides of the Atlantic, with surprising tenacity, though the gap between theory and practice is probably widening. The American Krapp (1927) records non-committally that many rhetoricians prescribe *so* after the negative, but that 'this rule is not strictly observed even by good writers, and certainly not by good speakers'. A few years later (1932), his countryman Leonard published the results of an experimental enquiry into the acceptability of 230 items of debatable usage, including 'He did not do *as* well as we expected'. His panel of over 200 judges (over half of them teachers of English or of speech, with the remainder divided among linguists, editors, authors and businessmen) agreed to the extent that over 75 per cent of them accepted the usage as either literary or cultivated colloquial English. This placed it in Leonard's 'established' category, contrasting with the 'illiterate' (under 25 per cent acceptance) and 'disputed' (between 25 and 75 per cent acceptance) classes. More recently Gorrell and Laird (1953) have found both usages accepted. The tolerance of Leonard's judges suggests that there might be more of wishful thinking than of detached observation in the recently published (1966) *Modern American Usage* of the late Wilson Follett; either Follett or one of the scholars who helped Jacques Barzun complete his unfinished text remarks that 'One of the oddities of American English, as compared with the parent tongue, is the retention in the United States of the shift from *as* to *so* when the statement is negative. Apparently without effort, workaday writers and persons otherwise casual in speaking will say: "This summer is not nearly so hot as last", whereas English speakers and writers use *as . . . as* throughout.' More plausibly, the Commission on English of the College Entrance Examination Board (1965) finds this shift to be 'well fixed in standard texts and largely ignored outside them'.

The British situation is not so (as?) clear-cut as Follett suggests. Nor has it received much attention. Partridge (1947) follows the Fowler brothers (1906) in restricting his comments to the rather special instances of *as far as/so far as*. He distinguishes between figurative statements, where *so far as* is usual, and literal statements, where *as far as* is used in positive sentences, *so far as* in negative. The smaller handbooks of usage—some of them in indistinguishable British and American editions—have tended in varying degree to favour the old 'rule'. Collins (1960) prefers *so* after a negative; Berry (1963) claims that observing the distinction is 'one of the marks of the careful speaker and writer'; and Lieberman (1964) flatly condemns 'not *as* good as' and approves 'not *so* good as'.

The persuasiveness of the strict rule by contrast with the actualities of even responsible practice is revealed by a writer to the *Times Educational Supplement* of 25 March 1960. He quotes a textbook of English for French students (Carpentier-Fialip: *L'anglais vivant*) to the effect that 'the only acceptable negative form of the comparative *as . . . as* is *not so . . . as*', and records that 'examinees have been penalized for writing "He is not as big as his brother"', while the Paris education authority for purposes of examination amended John Steinbeck's English to conform with this dogma.

It seems possible that some French students speak in a manner more English than the English, for the dogma has little strength left in this country. In our enquiry, this item was the most readily accepted of the fifty. Nearly everybody (95 per cent of respondents) accepted it in the two informal situations, and two out of three in Formal Writing. The high measure of general tolerance deprives of significance the reversal of the general pattern of acceptance by occupational groups, with teachers and examiners uncharacteristically more permissive than students and non-educationists.

ITEM 2. The audience was *very* amused.

The argument here is over the propriety of *very* (as distinct from *much*) before a past participle. For the purist, *very* is an intensifier; only qualities—and not actions—may be intensified, and therefore *very* can qualify an adjective but not a past participle. But is *amused* in the given sentence a participle or an adjective, or both at the same time? Past participles do sometimes lose much of their verbal force and become more or less completely adjectival in function. The correctness of usages like ours depends, as the *Oxford English Dictionary* (*O.E.D.*) points out, on 'the extent to which the participle has acquired a purely adjectival sense'. Fowler (1926) was daring enough to assess the extent of this development in a number of *-ed* forms: *tired* and *celebrated* were to him clearly adjectives, whereas *inconvenienced* and *pleased* were not. Admittedly there was a no-man's-land in between, and in any case Fowler complicated matters by introducing three other judgements—whether the word was used attributively or predicatively, whether it applied to a person or a thing, and whether it was marked by a 'tell-tale preposition' (e.g. *by*).

Not surprisingly, practical writers have not been unduly bothered by these distinctions. The *O.E.D.* allows *very* qualifying a past participle (used predicatively or attributively) as equivalent to *very much*, quoting instances from 1641 by, among others, Addison ('many very valued pieces)', Sydney Smith ('a very over-rated man') and George Eliot ('I am becoming very hurried').

Nevertheless, the old 'rule' has survived into the twentieth century with at least some theoretical force. In America, Krapp (1927) found it 'not without justification', though a counsel of perfection. The experimental study conducted by his countryman Leonard (1932) revealed considerable disagreement among the experts over 'The man was *very* amused'. An editor dismissed it as 'not used'; one British linguist found it 'good British English,' while another thought it 'would not be used by most good speakers'. The resultant classification was 'disputable' (i.e. accepted by between 25 per cent and 75 per cent of the judges). Wilson Follett (1966) has recently re-asserted the traditionalist attitude to this as to many other disputed usages. He recognizes that 'Speakers and writers seem to feel less and less sensitive to the idiomatic as well as logical difference between true adjectives (such as *sorry*) and adjectives formed from verbs (such as *disappointed*)' and admits that a few adjectives from verbs—*tired, drunk*, and possibly *depressed*—have shed enough of their verbal quality to stand an immediately preceding *very*. But, with these exceptions, it remains for him a fact that 'finer ears are offended by past participles modified by *very* without the intervention of the quantitative *much*, which respects the verbal sense of an action undergone' and that 'a careful writer would no more put down "I'm very delighted" than he would "I'm very lost" . . .'. This smacks much more of hopeful prescription than of realistic description.

In England, the traditional distinction has been sustained by Treble and Vallins (1936), Partridge (1947), and Barclay, Knox and Ballantyne (1945). Vallins (1951), attempting to discriminate between examples where the *-ed* form had lost and others where it had retained its verbal character, finds that *very* cannot be justified in 'While still at Oxford he became *very* interested in social questions . . .'. Others have been less sure of themselves. Gowers (1954) deplores past indiscriminate condemnation by amateur mistake-hunters of all *very* and past participle constructions. He distinguishes acceptable collocations with participles that are in effect adjectival (e.g. *'very* pleased'— and, presumably, *'very* amused') from unacceptable ones with participles that retain verbal force (e.g. *'very* inconvenienced'). In the doubtful intermediate zone he recommends avoidance of *very*. West and Kimber (1957) advise the opposite, i.e. using *very* in doubtful cases such as *'very* disconcerted'. More dogmatically and conservatively, Collins (1960) distinguishes *'very* interesting' as correct by contrast with *'very* interested', and Lieberman (1964) condemns *'very* changed', which should be *'very much* changed'.

Our respondents were not much (very?) worried by this usage, which was voted 3rd in acceptability of the 50. There was no very clear variation of attitude by different occupational groups, but the 'spread' of tolerance ranged fairly widely—from 93 per cent in Informal Speech to only 57 per cent in Formal Writing.

ITEM 3. **The conservative-minded are averse *to* making any changes.**

The debate here is between 'averse *to*' and 'averse *from*', with the etymologically-minded demanding *from* to reinforce the Latin sense of 'turning away' (and ignoring the fact that Latin *aversus* was followed by the dative case). The *O.E.D.* gives historical support to both usages, but seems if anything to incline towards *to*, on psychological (as against derivational) grounds. It remarks that 'The use of the prep. *to* rather than *from*, after *averse* and its derivations, although condemned by Johnson as etymologically improper, is justified by the consideration that these words express a mental relation analogous to that indicated by *hostile, contrary, repugnant* . . . and naturally take the same construction. *Aversion* in the sense of an action, which would properly be followed by *from*, is now obsolete.'

Insistence on *from* is at least as old as the eighteenth century, when, for instance, Knowles (4th edition, 1796) included 'averse *to* or *for* study' in his Alphabetical List of Improper Expressions. The Fowlers (1906) contrasted the *from/to* dispute after *different* (see Item 37) with the apparently analogous argument over *averse*. In their view, it is advisable to write 'different *from*' (*to* being 'the aggressor' in this usage) but 'averse *to*' (where *from* is the aggressor). H. W. Fowler (1926) went further; for him by that time insistence on *from* rather than the 'more natural *to*' had become 'one of the pedantries that spring of a little knowledge'.

In America, Lounsbury (1908) also defended 'averse *to*' as of respectable lineage. He pointed out that even Landor used it, despite the principle he elsewhere asserted when denouncing as improper the preposition in '*under* the circumstances'. Another American, Krapp (1927), classified 'averse *from*' as rare. Wilson Follett (1966) lists *to* and *from* as equally acceptable, and in England the balance has been similarly even. Treble and Vallins (1936) accept either preposition, defending *to* as analogous to the same particle in 'a*d*verse *to*', but Vallins on his own (1951) claims that current usage favours *from* rather than *to*. Partridge (1947) sits on the fence: '*Averse from*, though etymologically correct, is perhaps slightly pedantic.' Among recent guides, Gowers (1954) concedes that 'averse *to*' has good authority but rates 'averse *from*' as more usual; West and Kimber (1957), with different emphasis, reserve *from* for formal—as against ordinary— usage; and Collins (1960) goes further by rating the *to* construction as both common and preferable.

Some of our respondents referred to Latin as if that were the determining factor, though uncertainty sounds in the ambivalent remark that 'The foundation of this grammatical rule hasn't got its root in the English Language at all' and in the comment that 'We do not always use prepositions and affixes logically—or perhaps they may have their own logic.' Perhaps it was doubt of this kind that led a minority (10–30 per cent) to reject 'averse *to*', especially in the formal situations. With an average acceptance rate of 81 per cent overall, this usage came very high (2nd of 50) in the order of acceptability. This top position precluded a wide 'spread' between situations, but it was noticeable that the examiners, while as tolerant as any in Informal

Speech, were much harsher than the rest (only 51 per cent acceptance) in Formal Writing.

ITEM 4. **Traditional and *contemporary* furniture do not go well together.**

There seem to be three main ways of taking *contemporary* in current usage:

(1) The most fastidious user insists on the strict sense of 'at the same time, whenever that time might be'. Using the noun-form he would say: 'I was a *contemporary* of Jones at Cambridge long ago; our sons are now *contemporaries* there; our grandsons may well be *contemporaries* there years hence.'

(2) Since the commonest time-referent tends to be the present, *contemporary* often means just *present-day*, as in 'Contemporary politics are dull'.

(3) As one of our respondents reminded us, advertisers, the press, and salesmen have given the word the new sense of *up-to-date*.

Partridge (1947) accepts the tendency of sense (1) to yield to sense (2), arguing that the orientation towards the past is coming to be made by *contemporaneous*. The modern (contemporary?) novelist William Cooper, in a radio talk printed in the *Listener* of 16 November 1961, suggests that the distinctive third sense might be realized in speech by the pronunciation 'contemp'ry'—as when, for instance, quoting from a modish American magazine the tribute 'As contemporary as C. P. Snow and stretch-pants'. Despite the pervasiveness of American mass media, however—or perhaps because of it—resistance to the most novel sense is still strong, even in the United States. The distinguished band of scholars who completed Wilson Follett's *Modern American Usage* (1966) complain that *contemporary*, a useful word for a complex idea, 'has begun to chip and crack from careless handling as an absolute instead of a relative term'. They insist that '*contemporary art* is not of itself synonymous with *the art of today*', and consider the utterance 'When we turn to *contemporary* opinion' in the sense of 'today we think' a perversion of an indispensable word.

If our respondents are representative, resistance to this development is, in this country at least, less strong than to most of the other alleged mis-usages. Reactions were mostly favourable, though with fairly broad variations both by 'situation' and by 'occupational group'. The 70 per cent overall acceptance rate (4th in the list of 50) represents an average between high acceptance (70–85 per cent) in Informal

Speech and Writing and comparatively low acceptance (40–70 per cent) in the formal situations. Only in the examiner-group did a majority reject the usage in the latter circumstances. (One of them remarked austerely: 'I expect *contemporary* to be used in this context with either a smirk or a note of apology if spoken, or inverted commas if written. I do not move in circles where it is spoken plain or written plain.' Perhaps fortunately for candidates, not all his examiner-colleagues seem so strict—one, for instance, commented: 'A lost cause!') By contrast, students were particularly well-disposed to this item, and teachers were relatively more favourable towards it than towards some other items.

ITEM 5.   **The data *is* sufficient for our purpose.**

The ending *-s* (or *-es*) is so commonly added to English nouns as a plural marker that any noun without it is liable to be used sooner or later as a singular. It is therefore not surprising that a small group of plurals in *-a* borrowed from Latin (e.g. data, strata, stamina) and Greek (e.g. phenomena, criteria) are used—occasionally, often, or regularly—as singulars. The presence in the language of singular nouns ending in *-a* (e.g. replica, diphtheria, euthanasia) probably gives analogical encouragement. The strength of the 'singularizing' tendency varies with the strength of the various pressures operating. Analogy may be reinforced by a felt need for a singular form such as the originally plural form would satisfy, by ignorance of the original plurality, and by association with a singular meaning distinct from the original singular sense. On the other hand, the tendency may be reduced by insufficient demand for the new form or by familiarity with the source language. Thus *stamina*, with a metaphorical sense remote from the literal sense of its singular *stamen* and belonging to the category of 'uncountable' nouns which do not normally occur in the plural form, is accepted as singular without hesitation. But the singular uses of *strata*, *memoranda* and *phenomena* seem comparatively rare, perhaps mainly because both singular and plural senses and forms are needed and because 'native' words meaning much the same— e.g. layer(s), note(s), remarkable event(s)—are readily accessible.

Our word *data* is apparently well on the way to joining *stamina* as a normally acceptable singular. A marked need for a mass-noun (as distinct from a count-noun) to refer *en bloc* to a set of particulars and the growth of scientific and experimental work concerned with mani-pulating data (work increasingly done by experts with little or no knowledge of the classics) have doubtless expedited the development.

The American Krapp noted in 1927 that the plural form was 'not infrequently mistaken for a singular and used in the sense simply of information'. The sentence used by Leonard (1932)—'The *data is* often inaccurate'—elicited from his various groups of judges more disagreement than any other item in his enquiry; the linguists on average voted it 'illiterate', the whole group 'disputable'. But by 1951 it was possible for a book on English-teaching in America to include the singular *data* in a list of much-debated usages by then definitely 'established'. (Other such usages included 'It is me', 'due', and 'like' as a conjunction—see Items 43, 15, 44.) The very recent (1966) attempt of Wilson Follett to stem the tide of change looks forlorn. It is easier to agree with him that 'possibly we should think ourselves fortunate if we can escape *datæ*' than that 'on the evidence, it is too soon to say that *data* is slowly turning into an English singular like *agenda*'.

In England, resistance seems to have been rather more sustained, at least on the theoretical front. Fowler (1926) flatly ruled that '*data* is plural only' and condemned even the inconspicuous false singular in '. . . has furnished me with so much valuable *data*'. A generation later, Gowers (1954) re-affirmed this ruling. In between, Partridge (1947) discussed the issue more fully. While noting that American *data* might be either singular or plural, and while considering that *data* is usually collective, he still described the 'singularizing' as wrong. (He was even severer on parallel usages; *stratum* must be kept distinct from *strata* and, though the addition of plural -*s* to original singular forms was permissible—as in *memorandums* or *phenomenons*—it was an 'unforgivable sin' to perpetrate *memorandas* or *stratas*).

The instances that Partridge attacks (*this* data; the phenomena will not have been considered in all *its* bearings) seem to be flourishing more healthily than the principles they are alleged to defy. The manuals—e.g. West (1957)—go on insisting that *data* is plural, but examples of it as singular proliferate. A recent H.M.S.O. publication, doubtless written by a high-ranking educationist (Secondary Schools Examinations Council *Examinations Bulletin No. 3*, 1964), offers: 'From this *data* it is possible to construct a scattergram . . .' Even more recently, a Joseph Payne Memorial Lecture on *Education and Change* (by D. H. Morrell) advocates the collecting of a mass of information about the qualities expected of young employees, so that 'we could then analyse *this data*', and a reputable linguist (D. Crystal) has said and written: 'Much more *data is* satisfactorily accounted for if one postulates a scale of linguisticness for these features.' The same and similar usages are being promulgated by broadcasting. Within a period of ten days, BBC speakers have been heard talking about 'all *this data*' (in a schools programme on Statistics), about '*stratas* of meaning' (Cliff Michelmore, on 'One-Way Pendulum') and about 'mass *media* and *its* impact' (by a headmaster who also complained that 'mass *media is* selling not only goods but values').

Against this background, the high degree of acceptance accorded 'the data *is*' by our respondents seems less surprising than we, with our academic literary bias, at first thought. With tolerance varying from 82 per cent in Informal Speech to 55 per cent in Formal Writing (placing the item 5th in the order of acceptability of the fifty), the use roused less resistance than '*under* the circumstances' or 'the family *are*', and much less than 'it was *us*' or '*less* accidents'. The pattern of reaction by occupational groups was uniform in all four situations, but with teachers throughout more favourably disposed than they were (by comparison with the other groups) to the items as a whole. Notably, two out of five of the least permissive group (examiners) accepted the singular *data* even in the formal contexts.

A number of comments revealed uncertainties. Perhaps the most significant was that of the student who was uncomfortable about both possibilities: 'If *data is* sounds ignorant, *data are* is apt to sound pedantic and affected.'

ITEM 6. **The members of the team laughed at *each other*.**

It was assumed that reference to a team would point to the alleged distinction between *each other* (= two only) and *one another* (= more than two). Fowler (1926) denies that his distinction has either historical authority or present utility: 'the old distributive of two as opposed to several was not *each*, but *either*; and *either other*, which formerly existed beside *each other* and *one another*, would doubtless have survived if its special meaning had been required.' The *O.E.D.* supports this view by tersely equating *each other* with *one another*, and by recording that the latter, though now implying more than two, was formerly used of two only. Gowers (1954), like Jespersen before him, endorses Fowler's denial of any rule, but others take an opposite line. For example, Vallins (1953) refers to Fowler's 'rather perverse repudiation' of a distinction which had been defended by Nesfield and others. Partridge (1947) also defends the 'rule', not as an *ex cathedra* pronouncement, but as an economical device. Among those dismissing the point more cursorily are: Treble and Vallins (1936)—presumably the former rather than the latter—who find the distinction 'harmless but unnecessary'; Low and Hollingworth (1941), for whom it seems a fact of life; Collins (1960), who would like the distinction preserved despite its neglect by reputable writers and language-theorists; and Lieberman (1964), who condemns *each other* when used of 'five women'.

A similar, though possibly more extreme, fluctuation of opinion seems to have occurred in America. There, more rapid progress (if that is what it is) has apparently been made towards accepting *one another* and *each other* as simple alternatives. By the middle of this century it was possible for De Boer *et al.* (1951) to attest that 'present and past usage prove beyond all doubt' that certain pairs, including the one under discussion (as well as *shall/will*—see Item 48), are 'completely interchangeable in cultivated English'. But the most recent American guide consulted—Wilson Follett (1966)—seeks to put the clock back. After conceding that the tendency to use *each other* for two, but *one another* for more than two 'creates no obligation', Follett argues somewhat equivocally that it is sensible to preserve the distinction so as not to startle readers who are used to it. His argument that *each other* 'carries an inherent implication of the definite article (each *the* other)', whereas *one another* involves a sense of the indefinite article, which 'is in fact welded into *an*other, a pronoun essentially incapable of a plural', is less than persuasive. And we would certainly require evidence before agreeing with him that 'most readers will feel the ineptitude of, "The explosions (three) were touched off one after the other (another) in separate parts of the school"'.

Our respondents placed this usage 8th in the order of tolerance but its average acceptability rate of 59 per cent concealed a very wide 'spread'—from 84 per cent in Informal Speech to only 36 per cent in Formal Writing. Teachers (32 per cent) and examiners (31 per cent) were particularly harsh in the latter situation, and students (36 per cent) and lecturers (37 per cent) not much less so. The comment of one judge that he would accept the item only if it referred to a team of two, suggests that the 'true' acceptance rate might have been rather lower than the figures suggest. One non-educationist betrayed the possibly paralysing effect of linguistic prescriptivism by remarking that '*one another* always looks wrong, to me!'

ITEM 7. **We *have got* to finish the job.**
The question here is an old, familiar one. In what circumstances, if

any, may *to get* be legitimately used to mean something other than *to obtain* or *acquire*? Opinion, like practice, has long been sharply divided. At the beginning of the present century Greenough and Kittredge (1902) bravely denounced objections by 'martinets' to such locutions as *to get tired* or *to get hot*—objections, they said, which 'ignore all linguistic principles, as well as the facts of good usage'. Other Americans were less liberal. Krapp (1927), for instance, categorized the compulsion-sense (e.g. You have *got* to do it) as 'colloquial, verging on low colloquial'. Marckwardt and Walcott (1938), while noting that the *Oxford Dictionary* similarly labelled this *got* as colloquial or vulgar, took the citing of Ruskin, Disraeli, Dickens, Eliot, Wilde, Shaw, Trollope and others as sufficient justification for classing it with 'literary English'. The judges consulted by Leonard (1932) were well enough disposed for the usage to be rated 'established'; only a minority of English teachers (11 of 50) condemned it. Some years later Fries examined the various uses of *get* in the material (files of informal correspondence held by the U.S. Government) he analysed for his *American English Grammar* (1940). He concluded that 'although Standard English as well as Vulgar English does at times employ all the uses of *get*, nevertheless, the very frequent use of this word seems to be characteristic of Vulgar English'.

In England, P. B. Ballard (1939), in accusing teachers—deprived of formal grammar as a weapon of attack—of fashioning 'other weapons equally apt to deaden and stupefy', instances the embargo on *get* as one of the worst of these weapons. His vigorous defence of this 'luckless word' urges that its pedigree is beyond reproach, and he quotes many examples of its use by reputable men of letters. Most of the examples, it is true, are either of the 'possession' sense (e.g. Thring's 'person who does not use the sense he has *got*') or of the 'becoming' sense (e.g. 'He *got* married yesterday', which has just the right suggestion of capture!), but he also rejoices to see the Government's abundant and ubiquitous topical message that 'We've *got* to be prepared'. Hornby (1954) treats the obligational *get* as an occasional intrusion into 'have (got) to'. But the most recent handbooks have inclined towards categorical denunciation. Collins (1960), for instance, vetoes *got to* in the sense of *require to*, and replaces 'I have *got to* go home' by 'I have to/must/am compelled to go home'.

For the majority of our judges the question seemed to be less one of total acceptability or not, than one of level of acceptability. Only one other item (No. 17) produced a wider 'spread' of tolerance than this *got*-usage; acceptability ranged from 84 per cent in Informal Speech to 16 per cent in Formal Writing. In terms of general acceptability, it ranked high in the Informal Speech (4th of 50) and Informal Writing (11th) settings, but much lower (15th, 32nd) in the corresponding formal situations.

Rather depressingly perhaps—in that it might reveal a 'hangover' from classroom censoriousness—students were, at least in the formal contexts, the most hostile group, though teachers and examiners came close behind. Is this usage, one is tempted to ask, the sort of readily identifiable, easily marked item that attracts more adverse attention than 'errors' less easily isolated? (The suspicion is strengthened by a rather similar pattern of reaction to 'his family *are*'—Item 10.) On the other hand, the few who felt impelled to comment mainly defended the usage as having 'its own effectiveness', as sounding 'more urgent than *must* finish', and as striking a blow for freedom from 'traditional jargon and formality in the Civil Service'.

ITEM 8. **Young girls do not dress *the way* their grand-mothers did.**

This item was included less for any intrinsic importance (we were not aware that it occasioned much dispute) than for possible comparison with Leonard's 'He doesn't do it *the way* I do'. The responses of Leonard's panel (1932) put it in the category of 'established literary English'; he himself described it as 'clearly good colloquial English, but round-about'. Marckwardt and Walcott (1938) drew attention to the *O.E.D.*'s citing, in support of the usage, of Shakespeare, Addison, Hardy and others.

One of our respondents neatly added Thurber to this list on the strength of 'We have cats *the way* other people have mice'. Another probably expressed a fairly general feeling in calling the usage an 'American importation'. It may have been this feeling—however inaccurate its basis—that produced a high rejection rate in Formal Speech and Writing, with only 30 per cent and 17 per cent acceptance rates. These figures contrasted sharply with acceptances of 77 per cent in Informal Speech and 55 per cent in Informal Writing. These widely-spaced scores averaged out at 45 per cent. In terms of 'spread' the item ranked high—6th out of 50. The group of 35 examiners were as lenient as any in Informal Speech (74 per cent), but much more severe in Informal Writing (40 per cent) and the two formal situations (Speech 20 per cent, Writing 6 per cent).

It would seem that this item, though—or probably to a large extent because—it rouses little opposition in America, has a long way to go before being similarly accepted in Britain.

ITEM 9.   *Under* these circumstances no-one should complain.
Resistance to this very common locution comes from those who, insisting on the Latin sense of *circum*, claim that one can only be *in* surroundings. Landor, as already noted, was one of these literalists, though—as Lounsbury (1908) pointed out—he went on inconsistently to use 'averse *to*'. The *O.E.D.* formulates a nice but rather unreal distinction between *in* for 'mere situation', *under* for 'action affected'. Instances of '*under* the circumstances' are cited from as early as 1665.

In the present century opinion has wavered. Greenough and Kittredge (1902) record the frequent unhesitating use of '*under* the circumstances', and add that those who, encountering the very common 'under the following circumstances', prefer *in* to *under*, nevertheless 'rest undisturbed by the contradiction in *following*' (presumably, that is, between the notions of *following* and *standing*). The Leonard study (1932) concluded by placing our item among the 'established' ones (i.e. with at least 75 per cent acceptance). Marckwardt and Walcott (1938) grouped the *under/in* choice with other Leonard items involving 'shades of distinction entirely too subtle for any but the more fastidious of literary stylists to differentiate'. In England, Fowler (1926) dismissed the issue as puerile; literally, circumstances may include overhead elements (e.g. a threatening sky); and metaphorically the word means 'the state of affairs' and may naturally be conceived as exercising the pressure under which one acts.

Nevertheless, Partridge (1947) tries to revive the distinction, asserting of '*under* . . .' that 'this almost universal construction is strictly incorrect' and giving the astonishing advice: 'When in doubt use *in*, which is always correct.' Gowers (1954) supports Fowler; any appeal to logic is irrelevant, 'because, as cannot be too often repeated, English idiom has a contempt for logic'. At the same time, however, he claims the personal right—as a matter of taste rather than rule—to use *in*. Vallins (1953) also endorses Fowler's view, and even suggests that the *in* construction is but a 'proud variant of those who remember their "grammar" not wisely but too well'.

One of our university teachers rated *in* as 'decidedly unusual', but enough of the others seemed conscious of the traditional distinction to keep the acceptability rate down to a modest average level of 64

per cent, with a fair 'spread' between Informal Speech (82 per cent)
and Formal Writing (46 per cent). Despite the one quoted, college
and university lecturers as a group were comparatively less well-
disposed than usual and in fact displaced examiners as the most
resistant group.

ITEM 10. **He is in London, but his family *are* in Bourne-
mouth.**

This raises the question of concord; should a verb associated with a
'noun of multitude' be singular or plural in form? If there ever was a
strong tradition favouring the strictly grammatical singular, it has
given way in many quarters to a more flexible attitude. The choice
may be made according to semantic 'feeling', or even left completely
open. The Fowlers' *King's English* (1906) merely asks for consistency
within a single context—all singular or all plural. Fries (1940) found the
plural verb in common use by his 'Standard' writers (e.g. The family
occupy a house . . . The family *were* very fine people), though the
singular also occurred (e.g. The family *consists* of an invalid father,
etc.). On the other hand, his 'Vulgar' users rarely employed the plural.
His interpretation of the choice as determined by whether 'the attention centers upon the plurality of individuals embraced by the collective' represents the more or less standard theoretical view today.
The same principle is applied by Partridge (1947), who contrasts
'*Is* the family at home?' (i.e. the family as a unit) with 'The family
(i.e. the various members composing it) *are* stricken with grief at their
father's death.'

This comparatively liberal attitude was not reflected in the judgements of our respondents. An average acceptability of 47 per cent,
with no great 'spread' (67 per cent to 32 per cent), placed the item
14th in the order of acceptance of the 50. The main factor contributing
to this surprisingly low tolerance seemed to be—even more conspicuously than with Item 7—the adverse reactions of students, who
were the least tolerant group in all four 'situations'. Non-educationists
were also unusually hostile. But examiners proved the most tolerant
group for once. A possible partial explanation might be, not only
(as with Item 7) that the issue is a simple one to grasp and therefore
to be dogmatic about, but that it provokes in those who may be
educationally less sophisticated a rather naïve insistence on applying
an over-simplified grammatical criterion.

ITEM 11. The agreement *between* the four powers was cancelled.
The simplest form of the dispute is given by Johnson in his *Dictionary*
(1755): '*Between* is properly used of two and *among* of more.' His
wistful addendum that 'perhaps this accuracy is not always preserved'
is something of an understatement; the *O.E.D.* cites examples of
between referring to three or more from as early as 971 down to 1885.
In fact it goes further, casting doubt on any suggestion that the limitation of *between* to two has gained recent favour: 'While it is possible
that the last fifty years might have seen a change in the status of this
use of *between* [i.e. referring to more than two], yet its continuous
history of nine hundred years' standing would seem to militate against
this supposition.' The issue is seen by many, however, as a matter of
more than mere arithmetic. Gowers (1954) points out, for instance,
that, according to the *O.E.D.*, *between* expresses 'the relation of a thing
to many surrounding things severally and individually', while *among*
expresses 'a relationship to them collectively and vaguely'. Thus both
'the space lying *among* the three points' and—more relevantly for us—
'a treaty *among* the three powers' are unsatisfactory.

In America, Krapp (1927) endorsed the simple Johnsonian differentiation as 'proper' and even went to some lengths to explain away
'between you and me and the gatepost' as idiomatic or, better still,
as strictly correct in that the gatepost is not a third person, being
merely an emphatic indication that only two persons are involved!
His view was not strongly supported by the Leonard study (1932),
in which, though the judges as a whole had doubts and placed 'between
the four powers' in the 'disputable' category, the linguists among
them accorded it 'established' status. Leonard himself, in effect, affirms
the *O.E.D.*'s distinction by 'distributiveness'. He further notes that
the *New International Dictionary* gives 'A treaty was concluded
between the *three* powers' as an example of 'the proper use of *between*
bringing two or more objects severally and individually into the relation expressed'. Wilson Follett (1966) also rejects 'the standard oversimplification' of *between* for two, *among* for more. He argues that
'*between* is not merely allowable, it is required when we want to express
the relations of three or more taken one pair at a time. Thus it would
be hypercritical to object to *between* in the following: "The main
stumbling-block in the present delicate exchanges between Paris,
Athens, London and Ankara . . ." The exchanges almost necessarily
consist of *démarches* from each capital to each of the others, not of
identical and simultaneous messages from each to all.'

By contrast with these subtleties, the comments of many English writers seem naïve; they often consist of little more than asserting 'the standard oversimplification' with more or less primness. Thus Partridge (1947) states the simple rule (or myth) without qualification. Barclay, Knox and Ballantyne (1945) contrast dividing an apple *between* twins and dividing treasure *among* the crew. Treble and Vallins (1936) give similar examples but concede that 'in certain constructions the noun (after *between*) may represent more than two'— e.g. 'The choice lay *between* the three candidates.' Vallins on his own (1951) extends the concession much further; he sees (rather surprisingly) only the finest distinction separating '*among* the trees' from '*between* the trees' and contends that, since idiom and usage are stronger than etymology, 'a man may halt between *three* as well as between *two* opinions'. Collins (1960), however, is reluctant to defy etymology; because of the derivative connection with *twain*, *between* ought to be used only of two, though 'occasionally this rule is not observed'. To an example almost identical with that of Treble and Vallins ('—choice *between* four candidates') he adds: 'The air route *between* London, Paris and Rome' and '*between* ourselves'. The old dogma is re-asserted by West and Kimber (1957), for whom a conference must be *between* A and B, but *among* A, B and C. Berry (1963), too, allows no exceptions to the alleged 'rule'.

The few of our respondents who commented on the issue mainly defended '*between* the four' as logical or as inevitable in the absence of a reasonable equivalent. One speculated on whether this sort of 'technical' choice, especially when presented in an isolated exercise, 'brings out the pedantry in educationists'. This proved a palpable hit, for the non-educationists were distinctly more lenient than any of the separate educationist groups and half as tolerant again as educationists *en bloc*. Teachers and examiners were noticeably harsh, with under half of both groups finding the usage acceptable. Even so, with an overall acceptability of 57 per cent, it came quite high (9th of 50) in the order of acceptance. It is not easy to imagine that all or even most of the large number rejecting this usage (60 per cent in Formal Writing, 53 per cent in Formal Speech) would themselves write or say 'The agreement *among* the four powers . . .'. One rather curious aspect of the general reaction was that, with a comparatively low 'spread' (67–32 per cent), this item—by comparison with the others—was lower in the acceptability-order for Informal Speech (23rd of 50) than for Formal Writing (12th of 50).

ITEM 12.   **Answer** *either* **Question 1** *or* **Question 2** *or* **both.**
Here, as with Item 11, the point at issue is whether the given construction is strictly dual in number. If it is, then august examining bodies
(including some universities) are at grammatical fault in using this
kind of rubric. Their defence would doubtless be based on instrumental
effectiveness—a criterion increasingly acceptable nowadays. Strictly
grammatical or not, this usage apparently reduces the incidence of
examination-room misunderstandings.

The gap between theory and practice has long been recognized.
In 1877, for instance, a writer to *Notes and Queries* (5th series, 17 March)
held it to be 'wrong to use *either* or *neither* when speaking of more than
two persons or things', but admitted that doing so was 'almost universal'. Fowler (1926) included the attempted embargo among his
'fetishes' and quoted in approval '*Either* the idol of patriotism . . . *or*
conscription . . . *or* the fact that tramping was discouraged . . . accounts
for it'. The American Krapp (1927) defended the 'rule': '*either* and
neither are correctly used only when the choice is between two'. From
the wide disagreement over '*Either* of these *three* roads is good' among the
judges in his survey, Leonard (1932) concluded that this construction
'should probably be avoided on the principle that where usage is
divided, one is more comfortable on the conservative side'. Much more
recently Follett (1966) has also adopted a conservative attitude;
using *either* and *neither* with reference to more than two items is 'a
licence sanctioned by dictionaries and other authorities, but still
short of punctilious'.

A number of English writers on usage are quite dogmatic. Thus Low
and Hollingworth (1941) assert that *either* must be used for one of two,
and Collins (1960) flatly states that 'It is wrong to say *either* . . . *or* . . .
or.' Hardly less firm is Vallins (1951). After ruling that 'we cannot
write *either—or—or, neither—nor—nor*', he adds 'or rather, we should
not', so recognizing at least for purposes of condemnation Jespersen's
'neither in Shakespeare nor in the Authorised Version . . . nor in the
poetical works of . . .'. Gowers (1954) more equivocally suggests that,
if you decide to treat as pedantry the advice to limit *either/neither* to
two, you will find distinguished allies, including the Bible with its
'Neither death, nor life, nor angels, nor principalities, nor powers,
nor . . .'.

On average our respondents reacted with the same degree of tolerance (57 per cent) as to the previous usage, but more uniformly. Not
only was there comparatively little 'spread' (Informal Speech 67 per

cent, Formal Writing 46 per cent), but the various occupational groups stayed remarkably close to one another in their acceptances under the four separate headings and in general (the overall variance—between 53 per cent and 58 per cent—was negligible). Most comments focused on the examination context. One respondent rather surprisingly wondered whether examination questions count as Formal Writing. For others the construction was in this particular context acceptable, desirable or even essential, since 'extreme lengths must always be taken to clarify a candidate's choice'.

ITEM 13.   **It was not *all that* easy.**

The books have not had much to say about this usage; they vary mainly in how pejorative they make their classification. Krapp (1927) calls it a low colloquial speech form replacing *so*. In the view of Partridge (1947), the adverbial *that* (without *so*) is 'in England considered an illiteracy'; he advocates, instead of 'It's not that urgent', either 'It is not urgent to that degree' or 'It's not so urgent as all that'. He favours the latter as less stiff than the former (it could hardly fail to be so!); to some ears it probably still sounds stiff enough, though that might be in part due to the insistence on 'not *so*' (see Item 1). The implication that this turn of phrase is more readily accepted in America is made explicit—though still without evidence or authority—by West and Kimber (1957), who describe *all that* and *all that much* as Americanisms and amend them to *so much*—e.g. 'Does he love her *so* (*much*)?'

In our investigation the usage, with a general acceptability of 38 per cent, achieved a middling position (27th of 50) in the acceptance-table. As expected, the most conspicuous feature of its treatment was a very wide 'spread' (more than for all but two other items) between the extreme 'situations'. The 74 per cent tolerance in Informal Speech fell to under a half in Informal Writing and to very low rates (20 per cent, 9 per cent) in the two formal contexts. The student group was twice as lenient as others in Formal Writing, where otherwise the merest handful (including one examiner) were tolerant. This was one of the items which elicited an order of response by occupational groups closely resembling the 'average' order for the whole exercise.

ITEM 14.   **They will send the poultry *providing* the tax is low.**

Looking back now, we find it embarrassingly difficult to understand both how we came to devise (or perhaps borrow) such an odd-looking sentence and how we could assume that it presented a simple choice between *providing* and *provided*. The semantic strangeness of the utterance does not seem to interfere unduly with the usage issue, but the latter is revealed as complicated. It involves age and respectability, in so far as *provided* is sometimes thought older and better than *providing*; it involves the syntactic problems of 'dangling' or unattached participles; it has a part-of-speech aspect, in that—as Follett (1966) argues—'the obvious distinction is that *provided* serves as a conjunction introducing terms and conditions, *providing* as the participial modifier it patently is'; and a further element of choice is associated with both terms, in that they may or may not be followed by *that*.

The *O.E.D.* records very early uses of both forms, with and without *that*. The forms with *that* are older (*provided that*, 1460; *providing that*, 1423), but the forms without *that* also have a very respectable ancestry (*provided*, 1600; *providing*, 1632). Citations of *-ing* usage corresponding to our item are taken from George Eliot and Ruskin. In America Krapp (1927) accepts *providing* as used equivalently to *provided*; though 'less general and more recent', it has 'now gone a long way' towards correctness. The reservation that *provided* is 'appropriate only in formal statements in which a provision is distinctly made' (e.g. 'I will accept this office *provided* I am not required to serve more than one year') suggests that the *-ed* form would be suited to our example. Leonard (1932) used the sentence 'I will go, *providing* you keep away'. Though his judges as a whole placed it in the 'disputable' zone, the linguists among them rated it 'established'. In his discussion, Leonard quotes a British linguist who regrets that the *Concise Oxford Dictionary* 'does not, as I should, condemn *providing*', but concludes that 'With so decided a majority in its favor, and with such dictionary evidence to support it, it would be hard to justify any campaign to eliminate this expression from the vocabulary of school children.' Follett (1966) includes both *-ed* and *-ing* forms among his 'acceptable danglers', but recommends avoiding quasi-participles like *granting* and *providing* on 'the ground of accuracy or idiom or both; these two are best replaced with the past (passive) participles *granted* and *provided* in the so-called absolute construction' (e.g. provid*ed* only that the student is . . .).

In England, Fowler (1926) finds the *-ing* form often an unnecessary substitute for 'if'. Treble and Vallins (1936) also have reservations; though *providing that* is 'by no means uncommon in colloquial and in business English', it 'should not be used in writing'. Partridge (1947), however, for once does not side with the purists. He condemns 'a certain writer' for saying that *providing* (either with or without *that*) is misused for the conjunction *provided*. He adds fairly enough that *provided* was originally no less of a participle than *providing*. On the other hand, Vallins (1951) deplores that the past participle tends 'in careless writing and speech' to become present. Gowers (1954) wants stipulations to be introduced by *provided that*, which is better than the simple *provided* and much better than *providing*. Collins (1960) accepts both *-ed* and *-ing* forms as correct, but prefers them to be accompanied by *that*, while Berry (1963) revives the old dispute by condemning as 'a common error' the use of the *-ing* form as a conjunction.

Our respondents tended to be less sympathetic than we expected. Instead of figuring near the top of the acceptability-order, this usage came 13th out of 50. The 'spread' of acceptance in the four situations was wide (Informal Speech 70 per cent, Formal Writing 28 per cent), with all groups except the students voting quite heavily against *providing* in the two formal situations, and with examiners being particularly harsh (only 9 per cent acceptance in Formal Writing).

ITEM 15. **The performance ended early, *due to* illness among the players.**

Whether *due to* may legitimately be used as a preposition or adverb (corresponding to *owing to*) has been and perhaps is still one of the most contentious issues in usage. The *O.E.D.* quotes Johnson's view that the adverbial use is 'proper, but not usual' and finds it rare before the nineteenth century. According to the *Concise Oxford Dictionary* it is incorrect. In the eyes of Fowler (1926) it is worse than this; he stigmatizes it as illiterate and contends that the adverbial use of *due*, 'which must like ordinary participles and adjectives be attached to a noun, and not to a notion extracted from a sentence', is 'impossible'. Though he recognizes the tendency for certain participles and adjectives to acquire prepositional or adverbial force, and though he quotes a long list of examples illustrating how this is happening with *due to*, he nevertheless insists that recognition of the change should be delayed as long as possible—'perhaps idiom will beat the illiterates, perhaps the illiterates will beat idiom; our grandsons will know'.

The movement towards acceptance in America is strikingly demonstrated by the contrast between the results of two studies in which the usage was submitted to judges. Leonard (1932) found wide disagree-

---

ment, the item coming out at the bottom end—near the border with 'illiterate'—of his 'disputable' zone. Twenty years later the smaller survey reported in *Harper's Magazine* (1949) by Lewis found 65 per cent acceptance of '*Due to* the storm, all trains were late'. Theorists were similarly yielding ground. Whereas in 1927 Krapp found *due to* 'often incorrectly used as a conjunctive adverb', by 1942 Kennedy prophetically remarked that 'We may not like it, we may continue to check it on the papers of students, and yet we may have to give in eventually'—and this 'in spite of any logical or aesthetic arguments to the contrary'. Tolerance of the usage in schools was advocated in 1951, when De Boer and his collaborators advised teachers not to 'continue to check it in the papers of students'. The trend has, of course, not gone unchallenged. Wilson Follett deplores the remark in *Webster's New International Dictionary* (2nd edition, 1934) that prepositional *due to*, though objected to by some, is in common and reputable use, as in 'he failed *due to* faulty training', and rejects the notion that the 'unanchored' *due to* and other dubious usages can be validated by 'the doctrine that any locution in wide use is right by virtue of its mere existence'. But there is a note of desperation in the claim that 'the loose and lawless *due to* is still rare in writers other than those who take advantage of every latitude'.

In England, the retreating action has been and is being rather more stubbornly fought. Treble and Vallins (1936) distinguished correct from incorrect use by making it a 'good rule to use *due* only as a predicative adjective'. Partridge (1947), while conceding that the American evidence—as presented by J. S. Kenyon in *American Speech* (1930)—included 'numerous and impressive quotations', follows the *C.O.D.* in insisting that prepositional *due to* was 'not acceptable'. Vallins (1951) couples his condemnation with the observation that 'people who write letters to the editor seem peculiarly addicted to using *due* in the wrong place'. Gowers (1954) approves of the orthodox who still keep up the fight against prepositional *due to*, but gloomily forecasts that, now that the BBC has taken the side of Fowler's 'illiterates', they will probably win. West and Kimber (1957) fight on doggedly all the same, adding for good measure that *Due to* should not start a sentence. Whereas Partridge does not illustrate his charge that the misuse of *due to* 'may easily lead to ambiguity', Collins (1960) does. He suggests—very unconvincingly—that in 'I did not remain long after the accident, *due to* my being in a hurry' the reader must assume the accident to have arisen from the haste and—even more improbably—

that 'I did not visit the sales *due to* the wet weather' might mean that
wet weather caused the sales. Lieberman (1964) contents himself with
condemning, and offers 'because of' as the approved alternative. In
the same year Golding alleged that *due (to)* cannot be used adverbially
for *owing (to)*, but linguistic scholars combine against this verdict. On
the negative side, Halliday *et al.* (1964) record with disapproval the
persistence in G.C.E. Ordinary Level English examination papers of
questions requiring candidates to correct 'wrongly used' items such as
the Joint Matriculation Board's 'Due to his illness, he was unable . . .'.
More positively, Barber (also 1964), admitting that he himself shudders
at this usage, recognizes that it is 'now firmly established in this
country (it is used regularly by the BBC), and it is pointless and pedantic
to make a fuss about it'. Perhaps the fussers are not television watchers
and so miss the visual apologies ('Due to circumstances beyond our
control, the next programme . . .') which seem to outnumber spoken
equivalents on sound radio—perhaps because the latter suffers less from
technical hitches.

A suggestion that the movement towards acceptance of 'unanchored'
due to is, on balance, much slower this side of the Atlantic, might find
support in our figures. Whereas Lewis found 65 per cent acceptance
among his Americans of the 1940s, we found an average of 43 per cent
permissiveness, ranging from 61 per cent in Informal Speech to 27 per
cent in Formal Writing. However, in the setting of general censoriousness, this response put the item 19th in the order of acceptability,
near items like 'He *only had* one chapter to finish' (17th) and 'He is
older than *me*' (21st). There were no striking or unusual features in the
pattern of acceptance by occupational groups.

ITEM 16. **We *met up with* him at the Zoo.**
Though the argument about the legitimacy of tacking particles on to
verbs seems comparatively modern, the practice of doing so has long
been recognized. Logan Pearsall Smith (1925) applauds the enrich-
ment of language by the creation of what Bradley first called 'phrasal
verbs'. From such verbs—

> we derive thousands of vivid colloquialisms and idiomatic phrases
> by means of which we describe the greatest variety of human
> actions and relations. We take *to* people, take them *up*, take them
> *down*, take them *off* or take them *in*; keep *in* with them, keep them
> *down* or *off* or *on* or *under*; get *at* them or *round* them or get *on with*
> them; do *for* them, do *with* them or *without* them, and do them *in*;

make *up* *to* them, make *up* *with* them, make *off* *with* them; set
them *up* or *down* or hit them *off*—indeed there is hardly any action
or attitude of one human being to another which cannot be
expressed by means of these phrasal verbs.

The semantic gap between these phrasal verbs and the corresponding plain verbs is so much wider than that between *meet up with*
and *meet* that Smith might not have extended a similar welcome to our
usage. He might have anticipated Gowers, who—in *Plain Words*
(1948)—welcomes 'the marvellous flexibility' of these creations but
adds a warning against excess. Gowers quotes—with qualified approval—
a letter to *The Times* by Mr Henry Strauss:

> Must this government of illiterate exhortation continue to des-
> troy the King's English? Must industries be fully 'manned up'
> rather than 'manned'? Must the strong, simple transitive verb,
> which is one of the main glories of our tongue, become as obsolete
> in England as it appears in America? There (or at least in Holly-
> wood) you never meet a man, you 'meet up with' him; you
> never visit friends, you 'visit with' them; you never study a
> subject, you 'study up on' it.

Gowers himself is less caustic, though he does plead for watchfulness
against 'the infection which . . . is spreading across the Atlantic'.
This turn of phrase is omitted from his *ABC of Plain Words* (1951) and
Complete Plain Words (1954), where he confines himself to remarking
more mildly that 'the tendency to form phrasal verbs to express a
meaning no different from that of the verb without the particle'
debases the language without enriching it. He instances *lose out, rest up,
miss out on* as superfluous Americanisms, though *measure up to* may
prove a useful addition to the language by denoting a meaning different
from that of the simple *measure*.

Vallins (1953) also accepts a distinction between formations that are
tautological and those which contribute to 'the wealth and flexibility
of the English vocabulary and the richness of its idiom', but is more
liberal in his interpretation. He denies that some of the 'particle
verbs' listed by Partridge (1947) as tautologies really are so—e.g.
drink up, eat up—and differs from Gowers in accepting *loses out* as a
meaningful 'piece of intensification'. Vallins might well have been
one of those who see a distinction—albeit a slight and subtle one—
between *meet* and *meet up with*. The former could be a generic term for
the whole range of encounterings, while the latter might be restricted

to accidental encounters or meetings planned for time but not place (e.g. We expected and intended to *meet* him somewhere during the day and finally *met up with* him at the Zoo).

The omission of this usage from the Leonard and Lewis surveys and the absence of reference to it in most of our American sources suggests that it is widely accepted in the U.S.A. Only Wilson Follett (1966) of the authorities consulted mentions it, and he only as a brief item in a catalogue of prepositional uses. He allows *meet with* before abstractions (e.g. meet with rebuffs) but curtly enjoins 'no prepositions before persons'.

If there is a meaningful distinction in our item between the forms with and without particles, it is not one recognized by the great majority of our respondents. Even the most favourably-disposed group (students) in the most favourable situation (Informal Speech) mustered only 48 per cent acceptance. In the formal situations, acceptability was almost negligible—4 per cent in Speech, 2 per cent in Writing. This brought the overall figure down to 14 per cent and so placed the item near the bottom (47th of 50) of the list. Two groups (examiners, non-educationists) unanimously rejected the usage in formal contexts. Such comments as were made focused on the alleged American origin, suggesting that many people are very sensitive to and intolerant of importations of a kind they deem superfluous.

ITEM 17. **The instruments were *pretty* reliable.**

The process by which an adjective of 'full' lexical meaning acquires a comparatively 'empty' adverbial function (that of degree-word or intensifier) is by no means unprecedented. An example of a complete change-over of this kind would be the evolution of *rather* from Old English *hraðor* (meaning *more quickly, sooner*). Not quite so complete— because of the persistence of idioms such as *the very thing, this very minute*—is the development of adverbial *very* through Old French *verai* from Latin *versus* (meaning *true*). The tendency, both for the adjective to lose specific lexical meaning (it has long since lost its force of *cunning, clever, skilful*) and to indicate more vaguely *pleasing* or *attractive*, and for the adverbial intensifying function to gain ground, seems to be obvious enough. But how advanced is it?

To those who regard the degree-word *pretty* as yet another example of modern laxity and excessive colloquialism, it is something of a shock to learn that the usage has a long and respectable history. The *O.E.D.*'s impressive list of citations starts with Cooper's 'a *pretie* hardie

felow' in 1565 and includes Florio, Massinger, Fielding and Sheridan.
Fries (1940) adds, from Shaftesbury, 'I gave you . . . a *prety* full account
of all but her name . . .'

Nevertheless, the feeling that this use is essentially conversational
and informal was recorded in America by Krapp (1927) and in general
confirmed by the Leonard study (1932). Most of Leonard's judges
placed 'the catch was *pretty* good' among 'cultivated colloquialisms'.
In England, Partridge (1947) discriminates interestingly between the
pretty good/pretty well of 'standard speech' and 'lower-class colloquialisms
such as *a tidy step*'. More recent handbooks tend to record rather than
to comment, though Collins (1960) expresses reservations in that he
wants to exclude particular collocations such as '*pretty* ugly', '*pretty*
beastly' and '*pretty* pretty'. One can readily agree that the last—and
least likely—of these is diseuphonious as well as possibly ambiguous
(cf. pretty-pretty), but the objection to the first two may arise from an
unwarranted intrusion of the irrelevant adjectival sense.

With a general acceptability-rating of 39 per cent, this usage came
out fairly (pretty?) well from our experiment; it ranked 25th of the 50.
But the most conspicuous feature of reactions was a 'spread' greater
than that of any other item. Tolerance ranged from 84 per cent in
Informal Speech to a mere 7 per cent in Formal Writing, with a
very large gap at the Informal/Formal boundary (Informal Writing
51 per cent, Formal Speech 15 per cent). The extent of this 'spread'
was much the same for all the occupational groups but, rather surprisingly, the examiners were consistently the most lenient group.

ITEM 18. **There were *less* road accidents this Christmas
than last.**

The dispute here is over the choice between *less* and *fewer* for referring
to a number. Wilson Follett (1966), defying all the evidence that verbal
language is essentially arbitrary and man-made, asserts that *fewer* is
'by nature applicable to number; *less* is a word applicable to quantity'.
It is doubtful whether many students of language would endorse
this appeal to nature, but many accede to an alleged 'rule' to the
same effect, with the corollary that *fewer* qualifies a plural and means
a smaller number of. The authority for this 'rule', by which the use of
less with count-nouns has—according to the *O.E.D.*—come to be
'now regarded as incorrect', seems to go back no further than the
eighteenth century. Long before then, *less* was used quite 'naturally'
with countable items. The *O.E.D.* quotes the old English *læs* with a

partitive genitive in King Alfred's 'swa mid læs worda swa mid ma'
c. 888), as well as later uses by writers such as Caxton and Lyly; the
latter refers in *Euphues* (1579) to 'few Vniversities that have less
faultes than Oxford'. Such precedents did not, of course, discourage
prescriptive grammarians of the eighteenth century. Leonard quotes
from Robert Baker (1770) that *less* is 'most commonly used in speaking
of a Number; where I should think *Fewer* would do better'; it would
be not only more elegant but 'more strictly proper'.

In the twentieth century, Fowler (1926) endorses 'modern idiomatic
restrictions on the use of *less* and *lesser*'; he even favours changing the
use 'in quite natural speech' of 'to a *less* degree' to 'to a *lower* degree'.
Such a limitation would, in his view, make for precision. His advice
is repeated by Treble and Vallins (1936); by Partridge (1947), with a
concession to collocations with collectives, e.g. 'to wear *less* clothes'
and possibly '*less* people'; by Whitten and Whitaker (1939), who are
quoted verbatim in Gowers (1954); by West and Kimber (1957);
by Collins (1960), who reprimands the BBC for contributing
to 'a decline in correctness' by allowing '*less* than ten cases of
eviction'; and by Lieberman (1964), for whom '*less* students' stands
condemned.

Fowler's American contemporary Krapp (1927) does not agree
with him; he gives to *less* the meanings both of *not so much* and of
fewer, contrasting it with *lesser* (= *smaller*). Nevertheless, twenty
years later, the professional language-users canvassed by Norman
Lewis (1949) included enough objectors to 'I encountered *less* difficulties than I had expected' (attributed to Arthur Schlesinger, Jr.)
to produce a total rejection-rate (33 per cent) that ranked this usage
as the least acceptable of nineteen under consideration. The fact that
the sub-group of 155 American College Professors of English were a
good deal less lenient than the others (only 49 professors accepted the
usage) did not ward off criticism. One Geoffrey Moore (1959) con-
centrated on this 'barbarous usage' and a couple of others (different
than, the reason is . . . *because*') when attacking Lewis for interpreting
as 'linguistic liberalism' tolerance of 'sloppy English'. Follett (1966)
admits a few borderline cases (e.g. they work *less* than 150 days in a
year), but in general stands firm on the 'rule'.

Moore would presumably have got greater satisfaction from our
results than he did from Lewis's. By according our item an acceptance
rate of only 35 per cent, our respondents placed the usage in the lower
half of the order of tolerance (30th of 50). Both 'spread' (from 55 per

cent in Informal Speech to 18 per cent in Formal Writing) and the pattern of acceptance by occupational groups were near to the average for all items. Students and non-educationists were distinguished from the others by a markedly more lenient attitude (49 per cent and 38 per cent acceptability respectively), but examiners were harsh in all four situations (from 23 per cent acceptance in Informal Speech to 6 per cent in Formal Writing).

ITEM 19.   **Competitors should try *and* arrive in good time.**

Purists tend to insist on *try to*, on the grounds that it is illogical to both try *and* do something. But *try and* is not only given *de facto* recognition by some authorities as a commonly accepted idiom but is also sometimes defended as carrying a distinctive shade of meaning.

In America, Krapp (1927) characterizes the frequent use of *and* with *try* and a few other verbs (e.g. *go, come, send*) as 'well established in cultivated colloquial use' and 'occasionally found in lighter literary style'. Leonard (1932) notes that as a colloquialism *try and* was supported in the *O.E.D.* by quotations from Milton and Coleridge. It is difficult to sustain this limitation to colloquial respectability against the impressively serious quotations taken by Pooley (1946) from Milton ('At least try and teach the erring soul'), George Eliot ('to try and soften his father's anger'). Matthew Arnold ('to try and resist') and Froude ('To try and teach people how to live'). In fact, though the *O.E.D.* entry under TRY does designate this usage as 'colloq.', its treatment of the same construction under AND distinguishes the normal use of the connecting *and* after verbs such as *go, come, send, try* from the familiar and dialectal use after various other verbs. The very line from *Paradise Lost* quoted by Pooley above is cited in illustration of the former category. Whereas Leonard's linguists were favourably enough disposed to assess the usage as 'established' and one in ten of all judges accepted it as 'literary English', speech teachers rejected it. On balance, Leonard concludes that 'this expression is evidently perfectly correct for cultivated colloquial use'. Kennedy (1942) finds it acceptable for ordinary purposes, though he considers that 'when one really "tries *to* get something", he probably does a slightly better job'. The same shade of difference is identified by Wilson Follett (1966), who sees *try to* as 'unmistakably purposive' and therefore obligatory in such an assertion as that 'I shall try *to* climb Mount Everest', but who takes an uncharacteristically lenient view of *try and*, the very casualness of which makes it 'worth preserving for occasions when no definite time or effort of will is stipulated' (e.g. 'He knows we want one; he'll try *and* pick one up for us').

In England, Fowler (1926) postulates a similar but more subtle distinction. He considers that *try and* is 'almost confined to exhortations and promises' and that it can be justified in both these uses; 'in exhortations it implies encouragement—the effort will succeed; in promises it implies assurance—the effort shall succeed'. More persuasively because more simply, he also contends that *try and* is 'an idiom that should be not discountenanced, but used when it comes natural'. Despite this tolerance, the usage has been since treated, more often than not, censoriously. Partridge (1947) rules it to be incorrect and 'an astonishingly frequent error'. Vallins (1951) is one of the few who accept it; he finds Fowler's defence quite unnecessary and suggests that 'we take without question what the gods give, and be thankful that *try and* is beyond reproach'. The gift of the gods is none the less sternly rejected by Collins (1960), on the extraordinary ground that in *try and go* the two verbs are of equal importance and that therefore a person is to try and also to go. Collins also condemns 'Be sure *and* go', as does Lieberman (1964).

Our judges distinguished sharply between informal and formal uses, with very little concession to the latter (13 per cent acceptance in Speech, 6 per cent in Writing). Only in Informal Speech did tolerance rise above the halfway mark (55 per cent). Curiously, the pattern of reaction of occupational groups was almost the reverse of the norm for all usages. Examiners were for once the most lenient in overall reaction (34 per cent) and especially in Informal Speech (77 per cent), while the corresponding figures for non-educationists (23 per cent, 60 per cent) were uncharacteristically harsher than the rest. The final average general acceptance rate of 27 per cent seems surprisingly low for what many think a harmless and convenient turn of phrase. Perhaps this is one of those easily identifiable 'errors' that in questionnaire conditions attract snap condemnations, especially by younger people and by those normally less involved in the business of language-assessment.

ITEM 20. **The process is *very unique*.**

This usage probably offers the starkest example of conflict between lexical theory and actual practice. As long ago as 1902 Greenough and Kittredge remarked on the 'general tendency of language to employ absolute words (like *perfect* or *true*) as if they were relative, as when we "compare" absolute adjectives: *more perfect, most perfect, very true, more true*'. The word *unique* seems to be the most extreme (if *extreme* can be compared) in this kind. The dictionaries record the 'relative use' (the *O.E.D.*'s earliest citation is from 1809) but sometimes label it 'vulgar'. Those who consider the issue at greater length find things less simple. Thus the Fowler brothers (1906) insist that there are no degrees of uniqueness and fear that the same 'slovenly use' that has reduced *singular* to the weaker sense of *remarkable* will undermine another of the same 'depreciating series', so that 'before long *rather unique* will be familiar' and we shall have to concentrate on defending *unexampled* from qualification. They find some consolation in believing that such sentences as Charlotte Brontë's 'A *very unique* child, thought I' are still regarded as solecisms. Twenty years later Henry Fowler (1926) is still fighting the battle, though a hint of yielding appears in his delicate (and perhaps in the last resort illusory) distinction between adverbs that *unique* cannot tolerate (e.g. *more, most, somewhat, rather, comparatively*—and *very*) and those that it can. The latter include not only *absolutely, perhaps, surely* and *really*, but also some—e.g. *nearly, almost, quite*—that come dangerously close to the sense of degree. The difficulty of making this sort of demarcation is illustrated by the contrast between Vallins (1951), who finds 'a kind of self-contradiction' in *almost unique*, and Gowers (also 1951), who dismisses *rather unique* as meaningless but adds confidently that 'we can of course say *almost unique*'. Follett (1966) interprets absoluteness in the same way as Gowers—'something can be *almost unique* but not *rather unique*'.

Less discursive writers tend to insist tersely but categorically on the impropriety of qualifying an absolute at all. Treble and Vallins (1936) describe *unique* as a much misused epithet. Partridge (1947) rules that 'the frequent use of *unique(ly)* to express mere rarity or excellence is incorrect', adding severely that 'there can be no qualification of the absolute without a contradiction of the quality which it asserts'. Though Collins (1960) similarly insists that a thing either is or is not *unique*, he admits regretfully that 'through being used too often, and carelessly, it [*unique*] has to some extent lost its original meaning'. (One might fairly wonder whether *lost* is not also an absolute term and accuse Collins of equal carelessness in qualifying it *to some extent*!) Lieberman (1964) flatly condemns *more unique* and Golding (1964) asserts that *unique* has only the positive degree.

Barbara Strang (1962) has protested against 'popular pedantry', singling out *unique* for special treatment. She insists that it is no different from other adjectives of 'absolute' rather than 'gradable' meaning; they can all be modified by *more, most,* or the inflections of comparison, though the effect is to weaken, not to intensify, the meaning. For example, *more pure* means *more nearly pure, most pure* means *nearest of all to being pure.* This defence extends, of course, to *more/most unique,* but presumably not to *very unique.*

The apparent recent tendency towards uncompromising rejection is supported by the reactions of our respondents. With an average acceptance rate of a mere 11 per cent, this usage came out worst of the fifty (though not quite bottom of the list in any of the four separate 'situations'). One must, however, agree with a critic that 'this particular example looks odd'. The temptation to condemn, strengthened in any case by the test-situation, may have been reinforced by the lack of any context in which our sentence might have seemed likely.

ITEM 21. **He is older than *me*.**

Much of the responsibility for the tangled dispute about whether *than* can be used not only as a conjunction—e.g. 'than I (am)'—but also as a preposition—e.g. 'than me'—seems to rest with eighteenth-century grammarians. The argument might well have been initiated by Bishop Lowth (1762), who maintained that 'the English Language, as it is spoken by the politest part of the nation, and as it stands in the writings of our most approved authors, often offends against every part of Grammar'. His remedy was greater thoroughness in studying grammatical rules, so as to make the language less simple and consequently more demanding of scrupulous attention. An important area of study included the remnants of case-inflection and other affinities with Latin. For Lowth, *than* corresponds to Latin *quam;* it is therefore a conjunction and takes the same case after as before it, i.e. the nominative; the following nominal is seen logically as the subject of an elliptical clause—e.g. older than I *am.* Opposed to this alleged rule stands the language experience of centuries. The *O.E.D.* quotes examples of 'prepositional' *than* with an 'objective' case from as far back as 1560. The usage is, of course, very common today, and modern linguists attribute its persistence largely to the power of word-order in English. The order Subject-Verb-Direct Object is so common in English that first and third positions are strongly associated with 'nominative' and 'accusative' pronoun forms.

Here, one might think, is a situation where grammarians might forgo their preference for single favoured usages and tolerate both constructions equally. There is, as Leonard (1929) points out, precedent for such an attitude; 'William Ward . . . presents both sides of the question and permits either construction.' And such an attitude seems to have persisted at least until past the middle of the nineteenth century, when Dean Alford (1869) recorded as fact both ways of 'constructing a clause with a comparative and *than*'. With some subtlety he distinguishes between the more solemn pattern using the nominative—e.g. the Biblical 'My Father is greater than *I*'—and the use in ordinary conversation of a less weighty and formal construction, either the full clause (than *I am*) or the prepositional expression (than *me*). It is possible to go further and suggest that the logic of Lowth's case for the conjunctive *than* introducing a clause is dubious. Leonard's survey of eighteenth-century theory reveals that 'The ingenious Withers was the only grammarian logical and subtle enough to discover that this whole procedure of supplying a construction after *than* harbors a hideous error'; Withers pointed out that 'the Instance adduced by Lowth to corroborate this Hypothesis unfortunately subverts it—they are wiser than I am WISER'. By this argument critics of our sentence seem to demand 'He is older than I am old*er*'.

Fowler (1906, 1926) complicates the issue by adding another questionable argument in favour of Lowth's view. He finds a possible ambiguity in sentences with three personal pronouns, e.g. 'You treat her worse than me'. Spoken by an educated person (i.e. one accepting the 'rule'!), this means that 'You treat her worse than you treat me'. But from the mouth of an uneducated person it could mean 'You treat her worse than I (do)'. Fowler does not seem to recognize that his policy of supporting the 'rule', by his own argument, can help only the educated—who presumably do not need the help. In the circumstances it is hardly surprising that Leonard's judges (1932) found this usage (in 'You are older than *me*' and 'I am older than *him*') disputable. His linguists, as with other items, were comparatively lenient, but teachers of English and speech, as well as businessmen, were distinctly hostile.

Partridge (1947) takes an unusually liberal line. Not only does he prefer the objective pronoun and dismiss as incorrect Swift's 'You are a much greater loser than *I*', but he also deplores attempts by American grammarians to take the opposite line—on the grounds that 'school teachers have so much trouble trying to overcome the student's disinclination to use the nominative case in the final position'. Vallins is much more conservative. With Treble (1936) he includes 'He is as tall as *me*' in a catalogue of common errors. Both here and in his own handbook (1951) he blames analogy with the French disjunctive *que moi*, which in his view explains but does not justify the misuse. He does, however, concede that 'the use of the emphatic form (*me, him, her*) for the subject form is not to be too severely frowned upon unless it leads to ambiguity'. Gowers (1954) rather unhelpfully juxtaposes the *O.E.D.*'s rejection of the prepositional use (except *than whom*, which is stilted anyway) and the observation that 'Examples can be found in good writers, including a craftsman as scrupulous as Mr. Somerset Maugham'. More recent legislators—e.g. Collins (1960), Berry (1963), Lieberman (1964), Golding (1964)—have simply endorsed the conjunctive and rejected the prepositional use except before *whom*, without indicating why this last form should be exempted. (The examples quoted are almost exclusively of singular pronouns. It would have been interesting to present the less familiar plural construction, as used, for example, by Burke in 'There were Three Estates in Parliament; but in the Reporters' Gallery yonder, there sat a Fourth Estate more important far than *they* all'.)

A number of our respondents commented on various grammatical aspects, with a hint of unease at the tension between grammatical theory and usage (e.g. 'Often incorrect grammar sounds better to the ear than correct grammar'). Perhaps this unease contributed to the wide variation of reaction by 'situation': the 'spread' between Informal Speech (78 per cent acceptance) and Formal Writing (16 per cent) was one of the widest. Resistance in the two formal settings was about three times stronger than in the informal contexts. In the latter cases, lecturers—compared with other occupational groups—were much more lenient than usual, while non-educationists were much less so.

ITEM 22. **They work *evenings* and *Sundays***

This usage was included mainly because it figured in Leonard's enquiry (1932). Nearly three-quarters of his judges approved of the -*s* form as an alternative to the phrase equivalent (*in the* evenings; *on* Sundays), though in this case the linguists were less favourably disposed than the rest. These results support the view of Krapp (1927) that the 'genitive' form (which he likens to German *nachmittags*) is good idiom, at least in America. The *Oxford Dictionary*'s Supplement characterizes *evenings* as 'chiefly U.S. and dialect'; and Fowler (1926) quotes from the *O.E.D.* a remark on the use of a singular day-name without *on*: 'The adverbial use of the names of the days of the week is now chiefly U.S. except in collocations like *next Saturday, last Saturday*.'

The reactions of our respondents did not suggest any marked increase in American influence since Fowler's time. An average acceptance rate of 46 per cent made the item more acceptable than two-thirds of the total battery. Between the extreme 'situations' of Informal Speech and Formal Writing the range of tolerance—from 75 per cent to 22 per cent—was very wide, and the gap between responses in the two informal and the two formal contexts was considerable. Teachers, comparatively speaking, were rather more tolerant and lecturers rather less so than usual. Examiners were, throughout, the harshest; only 9 per cent of them accepted the usage in Formal Writing.

One judge who commented that there is 'no reasonably close equivalent' perhaps had in mind the cumbrousness of a construction using two different prepositions—'they work *in* the evenings and *on* Sundays'. At least the *-s* forms avoid such elaboration. It might be that this aspect was not much noticed and that judgements tended to apply to the isolated choice between *-s* form and adverbial phrase.

ITEM 23. They behaved differently at school *than* they did at home.

It is not possible completely to separate this usage from Item 37's 'Roller-skating is very different *to* ice-skating'. In both cases the issue is primarily one of choice of 'particle' after *different(ly)*. And in the two examples given, the distinction is clear enough between the conjunctive *than* followed by a clause and the prepositional *than* followed by a nominal item. But this distinction can be blurred by constructions where ellipsis may be alleged; the item used by Lewis (1949)— 'His work is different *than* mine'—is of this character, as is also the construction in which *than* is followed by an adverb (e.g. 'She seemed different today *than* she had seemed yesterday). We shall defer discussion of obviously prepositional issues to Item 37, but mention here not only clearly conjunctive constructions but also marginal cases.

Both the full and the elliptical clause constructions have respectable histories. The *O.E.D.* cites, from 1844, 'He seems to have spent his time somewhat *differently than* was usual' and, from 1665, 'Reason acts much *differently* now *than* formerly'. Many eighteenth-century grammarians tried to insist on *from* as semantically consistent with the *dis-* prefix of *diff*erence; some also allowed *to* (presumably to parallel *similar to*); but few could tolerate *than*. Leonard (1929) quotes from Baker (1770, 1779) a rule, 'repeated in countless handbooks for the next century and a half', that 'a *different* Manner *than* is not English.

We say *different to* and *different from*.' Baker, in fact, preferred the latter and wished to 'banish the expression of *different to*'.

The *than* usage has gained ground steadily, particularly in America. Krapp (1927) finds that *'different than*, though reprehended by the authorities and avoided by careful writers, may nevertheless be found occasionally in writings of good standing'. The distinguished linguist Sapir perhaps qualifies for this 'good standing'; a rather odd sentence of his (1921) reads: 'How differently our "I: me" feels *than* in Chaucer's day is shown by the Chaucerian "it am I".' Leonard (1932) chose an apt sentence to submit to his panel—'The British look at this differently *than* we do.' He was rewarded with an 'astonishing range in judges' placements', with over 15 per cent approving it as formal English, but about 50 per cent condemning it as illiterate. The item used by Lewis (1949)—'His work is different *than* mine'—might equally well be discussed as a prepositional construction, but may for convenience be mentioned here. He interpreted the favourable reaction of 62 of his 155 American College Professors of English as 'linguistic liberalism'. Geoffrey Moore, however, equated this with 'sloppy English', suggesting that the professors were undermining the good work of textbook writers. Robert Pooley (1946) could have been one of the professors; in his view present standards do not require objection to the phrase *different than*. Other American authorities have followed the same trend in varying degree. Gorrell and Laird (1953), for instance, record that *'different from* is the preferred idiom, although *different than* is recognized as common usage'. The controversial third edition of *Webster's New International Dictionary* (1961) illustrates the acceptability of the construction with *than* by modern American citations, contrasting them with the British preference for *to*, as in Churchill's (rather un-Churchillian) 'very different situation *to* the . . . one under which we live'. Wilson Follett (1966) makes the same distinction: after *different*, *'from* is preferred; *to* is British'. He recommends avoidance of *than*, to condone which just 'because it is sometimes awkward to follow *different* with the accepted preposition is defeatism'.

It does seem that in British English *different(ly) than* is not so serious a contender for recognition. But it does occur. Gowers (1954), for instance, records that it is not unknown even in *The Times*, from which he quotes 'The air of the suburb has quite a *different* smell and feel at eleven o'clock in the morning . . . *than* it has at the hours when . . .'. He seems to approve the condemnation this elicits from grammarians. Golding (1964) more explicitly rejects 'My name is *different than* yours'.

Our respondents mustered a mere 30 per cent tolerance, with only the students showing a majority in favour and that only in the informal situations. In the general order of acceptability this usage ranked 36th of the 50. In terms of 'spread' it came lower still, with a comparatively narrow range of acceptance between Informal Speech (46 per cent) and Formal Writing (14 per cent). Despite the compression of scores low down in the scale, the pattern of acceptance by occupation groups was very close to the average for all items. Students were distinctly more, examiners distinctly less, lenient than the others. None of the 35 examiners was prepared to tolerate the usage in Formal Writing and only one in Formal Speech.

ITEM 24. **He *only* *had* one chapter to finish.**

An enormous amount of ink has been spilled over the placing of *only*. The rule-makers have been unable to resist formulating the attractively simple prescription that it should be placed immediately next to the word it modifies (in the same way that adjectives should adjoin the substantives they qualify). There used to be in rhetoric a Law of Proximity, according to which notions thought of together should be uttered together, and the *only*-rule can be seen as a strict interpretation of this 'law' by applying it not merely to general structural coherence but to the juxtaposition of particular words. The fact that on occasion variable positioning of *only* can produce different meanings (e.g. 'She *only* attended in the mornings at week-ends', contrasted with 'She attended in the mornings at week-ends *only*') has been exploited by the precisians to the extent of insisting on invariable rigour in the exact placing of *only*. In consequence, large numbers of illustrious writers have been put in the wrong. The *O.E.D.*'s citations of the non-proximate *only* date from 1483 and include, for example, Dryden and Tennyson. Fitzedward Hall (1873) collected 400 instances from 104 authors.

A convenient starting-point from which to trace the argument is offered by the correspondence columns of *Notes and Queries* of 1887. In May of that year, E. Welford reports his conclusion, based on years of collecting grammatical blunders by writers, that the most frequent fault of all is 'the misplacement of the little word *only*. Take up the *Times* or any other daily paper, take up any weekly paper or monthly periodical, and you will be sure to find one example or more.' A few weeks later, R. Holland retorts that: 'It may show ignorance on my part, but I confess I cannot see much difference, either in elegance or in sense, between "microscopes were only to be obtained" and "microscopes were to be obtained only . . .". The same remark applies to the other instances adduced by Mr Welford.' In the same issue another correspondent quotes a 'rule of collocation of adverbs and adverbial adjuncts' formulated in Professor Hodgson's *Errors in the Use of English*: 'They should be so placed as to affect what they are intended to affect.' But the letter-writer seems to overlook the fact that such a 'rule' can be interpreted psychologically as well as logically and can therefore be invoked in favour of some separated constructions as well as of juxtapositions. A more helpful observation is that of the American Brander Matthews (1901): 'The proposition of *only* is really important only when the misplacing of it may cause ambiguity . . . The rule— if rule it really is—must be broken unhesitatingly when there is greater gain than loss.' This sensible attitude is endorsed by Fowler (1926). He condemns the pedants who press for logicality 'when the illogicality is only apparent or the inaccuracy of no importance'. He accuses them of trying to turn English 'into an exact science or an automatic machine; if they are not botanizing upon their mothers' graves, they are at least clapping a strait waistcoat upon their mother tongue, when wiser physicians would refuse to certify the patient'. He adds—what is too often neglected by prescriptivists—that, in speech, intonation can and does reduce possible ambiguity.

Wilson Follett (1966) asserts that 'the last word on *only* was uttered by Fowler forty years ago'. If so, it was last only in the sense that it ought to have been decisive. The dispute has continued vigorously on both sides of the Atlantic. Krapp (1927) debates the possible placings of *only* in the sentence 'He walked as far as the door', though his distinction between '*Only* he walked . . .' and 'He *only* walked . . .' (i.e. didn't run) seems appropriate only to written English. The unrealistic character of a great deal of generalization about uncontextualized usage is discussed by Leonard (1929) in connection with eighteenth-century law-making: 'The rules for placing modifiers were of course dictated by a general purpose of securing greater clarity: but when grammarians came to look about for actual instances, they rarely confined themselves to sentences which might actually cause difficulty or misunderstanding in their context, since such sentences are not really common in experienced writers. Instead, critics took the usual short-cut of pitching upon sentences of a fixed type, regardless of their clarity or lack of clarity. Sentences containing adverbs like *only* came in handy.' Such a sentence—and one would have thought a perfectly unobjectionable one—was Johnson's description of *narrate* as 'A word *only* used in Scotland'. The Leonard study (1932) used as its example 'We *only* had one left'. As a group his judges rated this innocuous word-order 'disputable'; but the linguists among them found it 'established', though one of the latter did make the engagingly paradoxical remark that 'The best English writers seem to go out of their way to misplace *only*'!

This paradox is given chapter and verse by Partridge (1947). So convinced is he that 'good' English is that which obeys rules and logic rather than that used by 'good' writers that he does not hesitate to include in his black list lines from a Shakespeare sonnet ('The summer's flower is to the summer sweet Though to itself it *only* live and die'), an alleged lapse by the normally 'careful' Coleridge ('The wise *only* possess ideas; the great part of mankind are possessed by them'), and similar instances from modern writers such as Chesterton and Wittgenstein (The latter's 'We can *only* substitute a clear symbolism for an unprecise one by inspecting the phenomena which we want to describe' ought, Partridge thinks, to be changed to '*only* by inspecting'). A much more discriminating and flexible attitude is shown by Leacock (1944), who finds the cadence of the same Shakespeare lines more significant than any alternative, and who quotes other examples where 'natural emphasis overrides strict logic in word order'. Sensibly, he finds no ambiguity in 'He *only* died last week' and even asserts that at times the 'wrong' placing is preferable. He strikes a shrewd blow at excessively atomistic assumptions, by pointing out that, in 'This is a tale *only* told to children', told-to-children is in effect 'one solidified idea' and that consequently the sentence has more meaning than the ostensibly more logical 'This is a tale told *only* to children'.

Lewis (1949), who is 'sure that this innocent adverb is circled and arrowed more than any other word in the English language', included in his test 'We only have five left'. With fewer than half (44 per cent) his judges favourable, it was rated controversial, though nearly two-thirds of his professors of English (97 out of 155) found it quite acceptable.

Among others who have commented on this vexed question are: Simeon Potter (1950), who defends 'I have *only* been there twice in my life'—at least as spoken in a broadcast—on the grounds that 'Language, after all, is more psychological than logical'; Vallins (1951), whose verdict is that in this instance 'logic and "grammar" usually give up the unequal fight against usage'; Gowers (1954), who observes that '*only*-snooping seems to have become as popular a sport with some purists as split-infinitive-snooping was a generation ago'—though on occasion serious ambiguity can be involved (e.g. Can the operation only alleviate or is it only an operation that can alleviate in 'His disease can *only* be alleviated by a surgical operation'?); and Hartung (1956), for whom 'placement of a modifier depends . . . not on an invariable rule of logic or grammar but on the speaker's full meaning', psychological and rhetorical as well as logical. Recent handbooks have been more terse and less tolerant. West and Kimber (1957) rule that *only* should come before the word to which it refers'; '*only* had two' should be rephrased 'had *only* two'. Collins (1960) with rather less severity allows 'as near as possible' instead of necessarily 'before', and admits that sentences like 'I *only* arrived yesterday', though careless, do no great harm.

One of the most recent as well as most dogmatic commentators is the journalist Marghanita Laski. In an *Observer* of April 1963 she concedes that 'in spoken English stress may sufficiently limit meaning to justify placing *only* almost anywhere one pleases', but insists that in writing the traditional 'rule' is not pedantic; we should distinguish between 'I *only* need two' and' I need *only* two'. From her prep. school lessons she recalls that *only* 'modifies what immediately follows it, unless nothing follows it, in which case it modifies what immediately precedes it'. Her distinctly odd illustration is 'The peacocks are seen on the western front', in which *only* can be inserted in eight different places to give eight different meanings. This versatility in the service of a rigid dogma she implies to be the only alternative to the current unawareness of how to place *only*, which 'extends right up to the pages of *Mind*' and which 'diminishes the number of things people are easily able to say and inhibits their capacity to say what they mean'. Follett (1966) is more reasonable than this, despite his normal conservatism: 'When a special exactness or emphasis is desired, *only* may and should be moved close to its partner', but 'otherwise its place is before the verb'. Insistence on what he neatly calls 'the officious *only*' can torture both sentence and listener (as in 'He died only yesterday'), and in any case is the prerogative solely of those who say 'Only God knows'.

One of our respondents defended our sentence because '*only* gets more emphasis (and better rhythm) in this *early* position'. But the general response was less favourable; an average acceptance rate of 45 per cent placed it 17th out of 50 in the scale of acceptability. Not surprisingly, in view of the clarifying power of intonation, the 'spread'

between the extremes of Informal Speech and Formal Writing was
very wide (79 per cent), but the speech/writing differential was none
the less as usual overshadowed by the informal/formal distinction.
Acceptability in Formal Speech (29 per cent) was not much more than
half that (54 per cent) in Informal Writing. The pattern of reaction
by occupational groups reversed the usual order of tolerance between
lecturers and non-educationists. The latter, with only 37 per cent
favourable response, were surprisingly hostile.

ITEM 25. **His eyes were *literally* standing out of his head.**
Is *literally* to be accepted as one of a number of adverbs (cf. *awfully*
tired, *terribly* impressed) which have come to be used—instead of or in
addition to their orthodox sense—as intensifiers? If so, is such a use
legitimate always or only in colloquial exchanges? Does our usage
differ in essence from the use of *pretty* as a degree-word (e.g. Item 17,
pretty reliable), or is there a special objection to the non-literal use of
the particular word *literal*? Fowler (1926) takes the latter view: 'We
have come to such a pass with this emphasizer that when the truth
would require us to insert with a strong expression "not literally, but
in a manner of speaking", we do not hesitate to insert the very word
we ought to be at pains to repudiate.' If he is right in arguing that
'such false coin makes honest traffic in words impossible', we must
sadly record that verbal dishonesty is not uncommon, for the metaphorical use of *literally* seems to occur with increasing frequency.
     Nevertheless, nearly all the authorities condemn the practice. The
O.E.D. recognizes *literally* only 'in the literal sense'. Krapp (1927)
exemplifies the incorrect use in colloquial speech with 'He *literally*
hugged himself for joy', and Partridge (1947) with the 'slovenly
colloquialism' of 'He *literally* turned the house upside down'. As
Gowers (1954) remarks, a good deal of fun has been made of the metaphorical use of *literally*. His own contributions are—from a tennis
context—'Miss X *literally* wiped the floor with her opponent' and a
newspaper report that Mr Gladstone had sat throughout a debate
literally glued to the Treasury Bench—on which Punch's gloss was:
'"That's torn it," said the Grand Old Man, as he *literally* wrenched
himself away to dinner.' Wilson Follett (1966) wonders that writers
have not desisted—'in sheer weariness of listening to the injunction'—
from such mistakes as 'He was *literally* speechless. He could only murmur
"Good God!"'
     Ridicule seems, however, to have been no more effective than flat

dismissals such as those in the recent handbooks of West and Kimber
(1957) and Collins (1960). In fact, some theoretical defence is mounted
by modern descriptive linguists. Halliday *et al.* (1964), for instance,
deplore a G.C.E. Ordinary Level question requiring candidates to
correct the word 'wrongly used' in 'The girl literally flew down the
road'. Whether we like it or not, this defence may represent a more
realistic appraisal of the usage than the battery of condemnations.

Our respondents were perhaps not quite as hostile as we might have
expected. The item, with 35 per cent acceptances, came 31st in the
acceptability-order. This 35 per cent came from a fairly wide range of
reactions; the whole group varied between 58 per cent tolerance in
Informal Speech to 16 per cent in Formal Writing, and these figures
conceal considerable further variations between groups. More than
half the students tolerated the usage (79 per cent in Informal Speech,
27 per cent in Formal Writing), and the non-educationists recorded
62 per cent acceptance in Informal Speech. At the other extreme,
only ten (28 per cent) of the thirty-five examiners allowed the use in
Informal Speech, and a mere two in Formal Writing. It was, in fact,
an examiner who daringly pontificated that this is 'not so much a
matter of usage but of inaccuracy which will always be wrong'. It is
easier to sympathize with the non-educationist who thought that 'it is
the legitimate business of any teacher to discourage such misuse'—even
if discouragement, it seems, might prove nothing more than a retreating action.

ITEM 26. **They invited my friends and *myself.***

The use of *myself* (rather than *me*) where neither reflexive nor emphatic
sense is intended is probably a less disputed issue than most of our
items. It was included mainly for comparison with the responses—
over thirty years ago—of the judges consulted by Leonard (1932),
who used this same sentence. Though the *O.E.D.* records a long history
(1205–1856) of preference for *myself* 'in an enumeration, when not
occupying first place', only 62 per cent of Leonard's judges approved
of it. Leonard himself concludes that 'while people who are especially
careful of their speech would avoid this expression, nevertheless it
would hardly be safe to condemn it as incorrect'.

Partridge (1947) rules that the tendency to employ *-self* pronouns
where the simple personal pronouns are sufficient is to be resisted,
but the actual 'misuses' he quotes ('You and myself will . . .', 'Herself
and himself will . . .', 'He sent the enquiry to yourself') are not parallel

to our item. Gorrell and Laird (1953), on the other hand, do use an
exact parallel in 'They invited Anne and *myself*'; they suspect this
may be 'a mistaken effort to avoid the choice between *I* and *me*',
and favour '. . . invited Anne and *me*' instead. Their American countryman Pooley (1960) is more tolerant; in fact, he includes 'objection
to *myself* as a polite substitute for *me*' in a list of prescriptions which
survive in 'the less enlightened textbooks' but should *not* be endorsed
by schools. In an earlier work (1946) Pooley defended this very sentence of Leonard's against the charge that to use *myself* so is 'ridiculous
practice', since one would say 'They invited myself'. He rejected this
confusion of single-object and compound-object constructions and
went on to argue that, whereas the *me* form in an enumeration of this
kind was 'direct, forceful, and subjective', the *myself* usage was felt to
be 'modest, polite, and courteous'.

It may be that in England a more conservative attitude still pre-
vails. Certainly our respondents were less than friendly towards the
myself item. With a general acceptability rate of only 33 per cent it
came rather low in the table of acceptance (33rd of the 50). In Informal
Speech almost exactly half of each occupational group registered
tolerance, with teachers (52 per cent) the most and examiners (46
per cent) the least lenient. The decline in favour through Informal
Writing to the formal situations was fairly sharp, except with students
and non-educationists. One critic thought that *myself* might somewhat
remedy the lack of 'body' in *me*. Perhaps a more serious stylistic
consideration is that the collocation '*my* friends and *myself*' sounds
cumbersome to the mind's ear; a different example (e.g. 'invited
John and myself') might have provoked less opposition.

ITEM 27. **What are the chances of *them* being found out?**

Purists would prefer '*their* being found out', a construction which
would identify *being* as a word with noun-quality. This amendment,
it is argued, would remove the objection that it is not clear whether
of governs *them* or *being found out*. As it stands, *being* looks like a participle
and seems to combine in a vague way with *them* to form a unit which
the brothers Fowler designated—in order to condemn—a 'fused
participle'. As Gowers (1954) remarks, the issue is 'not in itself a matter
of any great interest or importance. But it is notable as having been
the occasion of a battle of the giants, Fowler and Jespersen.' The
ten pages of learned argument in *The King's English* (1906) led to
formidable criticism by the Dane and a defence by H. W. Fowler in

two Tracts of the Society for Pure English. Unabashed, Fowler re-
stated the case for the prosecution in *Modern English Usage* (1926).
To him, the fused participle resembled the clumsy German 'article-
&-noun sandwich' (e.g. 'The since 1914 owing to the world-war
befallen destruction of capital'), except that the latter, though ridiculed,
is grammatically sound, whereas the fused participle is indefensible
because it defies grammatical analysis. He recognizes that, willy-nilly,
the construction has gained so much ground that 'it is perhaps beyond
hope for a generation that regards *upon you giving* as normal English to
recover its hold upon the truth that grammar matters', but urges none
the less that every just man should join most good writers in abstaining
from fusion, thereby helping to retard 'the progress of corruption'.

The *O.E.D.* reports that the possessive form began to be dropped
as early as 1600 with names of things and with 'phraseological or
involved denominations'. (The example it gives of the latter—'in
default of *one or other* being accepted'—is clear enough, but its example
of the former looks very dubious; it is hard to identify a 'fused participle'
in the reference to Macbeth's witches as recognized 'by each at once
her choppie *finger* laying upon her skinnie lips'.) The Dictionary adds
that the *'s* is also commonly omitted in current spoken English from all
nouns and from emphatic pronouns, and even, in dialect, from a
pronoun standing before a gerund. Elsewhere, however, the possessive
pronoun and the 'single personal substantive' have retained the *'s*
form. At work in favour of the shortening is the influence of analogy
with the present participle: 'John was digging the potatoes' and 'Who
saw John digging potatoes?' have encouraged 'Who ever heard of
John (= John's) digging potatoes?'

Leonard's survey of eighteenth-century doctrines (1929) adds the
complication that at one time the possessive form was actually denounced as incorrect. It was the object of 'severe repudiation' by George
Harris (1752), who deplored the *'s* in 'Doctrine of a future *state's* being
taught' and added cuttingly that '*This's being done* would mark a man
of no education'. Even Lowth, in his second edition (1763), spoke of
expressions like 'The Rule's being observed' and 'its being disregarded'
as 'anomalies to be rooted out'. Lowth's objection is not (as it was
with some nineteenth-century grammarians) to the impropriety of
possession by an inanimate object, but to the 'amphibious' verbal
item which both governs an object and takes a possessive. As Fowler
did later, he appeals to susceptibility to grammatical analysis, but to
diametrically opposed effect; it is not possible, he argues, to resolve

'the rule's being observed' into 'the being observed of the rule'. Other grammarians and rhetoricians of the time—as Leonard illustrates—could be less dogmatic: Priestley (1761) admits either possessive or accusative, and Campbell (1776) thinks the possessive usage ought not to be entirely repudiated. The first writer to insist on the genitive is said to be Baker (1779), who demands 'His *words*' being applicable. Webster (1789), too, wants the genitive every time; this is 'the genuine English idiom', neglect of which often leads to ambiguity. Lindley Murray (1795) is more tentative, but his nineteenth-century successors adopted a firmly dogmatic attitude.

In his enquiry (1932) Leonard included three instances of the usage in question, including our actual sentence. All three were ranked as 'disputable', though the one involving a proper noun ('. . . the reason for *Bennett* making that disturbance') raised less opposition than the others, which used pronouns. For our item, Leonard concluded that 'while passable for the most informal English, it is to be avoided'. A decade later, another American—C. C. Fries (1940)—also found a distinction in practice between nominal and pronominal constructions. Whereas from his evidence 'it would be natural to conclude that the inflected form of nouns is *not* the normal practice before gerunds in Standard English', the situation was different with pronouns. There, 52 per cent of his Standard English cases had the genitive form of the pronoun before the verbal. Even in his 'Vulgar English' letters there was, to a slightly smaller degree, the same differentiation. Gorrell and Laird (1953), however, prescribed the possessive form (e.g. *their* playing poker) as possibly making meaning more precise.

In England, Vallins (1951) is not very helpful. Not even a conscience stirred by Fowler can, he admits, insist on the possessive in 'One has sad memories of parties of weary and bored *children being* endlessly trailed and lectured . . .' or in '. . . without *Mr Porteous or any of us being* able to . . .'. All the same, he finds the fused participle misleading and therefore to be condemned. Gowers (1954) is also rather tentative, appealing to our feeling that sometimes the one, sometimes the other, construction is idiomatic. His examples—'*his* (not he) coming surprised me', '*Smith's* coming surprised me'—are safe enough, but hardly support a generalization prohibiting, say,' I heard of *him* coming' or Leonard's 'reason for *Bennett* making that disturbance', where the possessives are not so obviously preferable. Hornby (1954) more reasonably accepts either pronominal form in 'I cannot understand *his/him* behaving like that', but more recent handbooks have tended to reinstate the old dogma. Collins (1960), though admitting a difference between 'I admired *you* running today' and 'I admired *your* running today', finds fault with 'I dislike *you* singing' and 'I was sorry to hear of *him* losing his shop'. Berry (1963) wants '*his* going' and Golding (1964) asserts that 'a gerund can be preceded either by a possessive adjective or by a noun in the possessive case, but never by a personal pronoun'. Most recently, however, the American handbook of Wilson Follett (1966) has at some length argued that 'there is room for both constructions, that the choice between them can express a shade of meaning, and that the fused form can be grammatically defended as a "heavy apposition"'. The criterion applied discriminates between the allowable 'But with the situation the way it is and *me* deciding to cut loose . . .' or (from an advertisement) 'To Stop *You* Skidding', and the unacceptable 'I'm strongly in favour of *you* putting someone on to tail the young lady' or '. . . without *it* doing them much harm'.

For our judges this was a 'middling' item; an overall acceptance of 40 per cent placed it about half-way down the acceptance table (23rd of 50). The 40 per cent represents a compromise between widely spread responses in the various situations. Over half of each group (from 81 per cent students to 51 per cent examiners) allowed the usage in Informal Speech, but far fewer (27 per cent students, 3 per cent examiners) tolerated it in Formal Writing. The pattern of group-acceptance was in all situations identical with the norm.

ITEM 28. **Intoxication is *when* the brain is affected by certain stimulants.**

This is another of the items included mainly for comparison with the findings of Leonard, who used the same sentence. In his survey (1929) of eighteenth-century notions of correctness, Leonard notes that this construction was disapproved of by Robert Baker (1770), who seemed to think that it contravened a principle of concord between a subject and a predicative nominative. Despite any theory, the usage was earlier employed even by grammarians; Greenwood (1711) has 'A compound sentence is *when* . . .' and Lowth (1762) writes that 'An explicative sentence is, *when* a thing is said . . .'. And, of course, this usage has persisted ever since.

Leonard's enquiry (1932) placed it in the 'disputable' category, with most linguists admitting it as colloquial English but with four-fifths of the teachers rating it 'uncultivated'. In England, this locution has attracted little attention. Partridge (1947), quoting 'Quadratics is *when* the highest power of the unknown is a square', remarks that '*is when* is a stupid beginning for a definition'. More recently Collins (1960) has endorsed this view, stigmatizing as wrong 'An opera *is when* the dialogue in a play is sung' and 'Hyperbole *is when* we exaggerate'.

Our judges tended to be less tolerant than we expected. An acceptance rate of only 37 per cent put this item in the lower half of the accept-ability-table (28th of 50). This was not due, as some might suppose, to any special harshness on the part of teachers; in fact, though the order of group-acceptance was near the average for all items, here teachers were a little more lenient than lecturers, at least in the informal situations.

ITEM 29. Their success, his attitude *inferred*, was due to his own efforts.

ITEM 45. He told me the story and I *implied* a great deal from it.

These two items are best treated together, since the point at issue is the alleged confusion between the meanings of the italicized words. Though the conservative-minded seem to suggest that they are a symmetrically contrasting pair, in fact there is long historical precedent for *infer* in the sense of the purists' *imply*, but not vice versa. Wilson Follett (1960) reminds us that '*infer* once meant exactly what *imply* means now—it is generally, perhaps always, so used in the seventeenth-century plays of John Ford'. Milton (*Paradise Lost*, Book VIII, lines 90–91) has 'Consider, first, that great Or bright *infers* not excellence'. And the *Concise Oxford Dictionary* gives *imply* as a secondary sense of *infer* (though not the reverse). The third edition (1961) of *Webster's New International Dictionary*, instead of repeating the note in the second edition (1934) of a use of *infer* as 'loosely and erroneously, to imply', omits the warning and twice under *infer* advises 'compare *imply*'. (This and many other 'liberalisms' have attracted a great deal of harsh criticism, from Dwight Macdonald and others.)

History and 'liberalism' notwithstanding, there seems to have been, until fairly recent years, what Follett calls 'a clear differentiation whereby *imply* goes with the transmitting end and *infer* with the receiving end of the same process of deduction'. He illustrates the contrast by suggesting that, whereas smoke *implies* fire, when you smell smoke you *infer* fire. Certainly the complaints about blurring this distinction have accumulated over the past thirty years. Treble and Vallins (1936) report 'a tendency for *imply* to usurp the meaning and use of *infer*'.

Partridge (1947) quotes two dictionaries—Nuttall and Chambers—in support of the distinction and deplores the misuse in a contemporary novel of 'Travers sent a report which *inferred* we were all blockheads'. Gowers (1954) also thinks the distinction worth preserving, though he admits that 'there is authority for *infer* in the sense of *imply*'. Richards (1955) associates the *imply/infer* confusion with that between *dis-* and *un-interested* (see Item 33) as examples of 'a degradation of the language'. Milton, he hints, would have done better to use *imply*. The fact that distinguished writers did not observe the distinction no more justifies the merging of the two terms 'than a general habit of promiscuity would show that to be good'. Some modern handbooks (e.g. West, 1957; Collins, 1960; Lieberman, 1964) have erected this argument into a dogma.

In our investigation, Item 29 (*inferred* for *implied*) was among those showing the narrowest overall variation of reaction between Informal Speech and Formal Writing, though it did elicit very diverse responses from the different occupational groups. The average order of acceptability (37 per cent) balanced an acceptance rate of 57 per cent by students against one of 11 per cent by examiners. Even wider disparities were found in different 'situations'—in Informal Speech, 68 per cent approval by students against 17 per cent by examiners; in Formal Writing, 51 per cent students, 6 per cent examiners. In the table of acceptability for all fifty items, this one came 29th.

Item 45 (*implied* for *inferred*) was even more unpopular. Its overall 12 per cent acceptability derived from the narrowest spread of all items—from Informal Speech 16 per cent to Formal Writing 8 per cent. Such heavy disapproval allowed little variation among occupational groups.

ITEM 30. **He refused *to even think* of it.**
Few arguments about usage fail to raise the question whether or in what circumstances it is permissible to insert anything between the infinitive-marker *to* and the verb-form itself. As Follett (1966) remarks, 'Like parallel fifths in harmony, the split infinitive is the one fault that everybody has heard about and makes a great issue of avoiding and reproving in others.' Everybody, that is, in comparatively recent times. As Barbara Strang (1962) puts it: 'Fussing about split infinitives is one of the more tiresome pastimes invented by nineteenth-century prescriptive grammarians.'

Protests against this fuss are not new. At the turn of the century

Brander Matthews (1901) pointed out 'that the Split Infinitive has a most respectable pedigree, and that it is rather the protest against it which is the novelty . . .'. Similarly, in a whole chapter on '*To* and the Infinitive', Lounsbury (1908) recorded that 'more than twenty years ago the late Fitzedward Hall—that terror of those indulging in loose and unfounded assertions about usage—showed conclusively that the practice of inserting words between the preposition and the infinitive went back to the fourteenth century, and that to a greater or less degree it has prevailed in every century since'. Hall's catalogue of examples, with some supplementation by Lounsbury, came from a galaxy of writers, including Wycliffe, Tyndale, Coleridge, Donne ('specially addicted to the usage'), Goldsmith, George Eliot, Burns, and Browning. Macaulay, in revising an article in 1843, even changed 'in order fully to appreciate . . .' to 'in order to fully appreciate'. Nevertheless, Lounsbury suggests that it is fair to assume that in previous centuries the great majority of the best writers of our literature never took kindly to 'splitting' and that objections to it increased commensurately with its frequency in the nineteenth century. In support of the latter contention he quotes twice from Andrew Lang. In his *Life of Sir Stafford Northcote*, Lang describes how, in negotiating a treaty with the United States, the British Government was willing to make concessions about the Alabama claims, the Canadian fisheries, and the like, but 'telegraphed that in the wording of the treaty it would under no circumstances endure the insertion of an adverb between the preposition *to* . . . and the verb'. Lang's other and more facetious contribution was in a lecture in 1890 on *How to Fail in Literature*; he advises anyone aiming at 'such a desirable result' that he cannot be too reckless of grammar, and that such recklessness might well take the form of always placing adverbs and other words between *to* and the infinitive. On the theoretical aspect, Lounsbury argues that, far from 'splitting' being a novel degradation, it was the original practice of joining *to* to the simple infinitive that was the corruption, for 'in our early speech *to* belonged strictly to the gerund, or, as it was sometimes called, the dative case of the infinitive'.

In England at about the same time the Fowlers (1906) were taking a similar line. The split infinitive in their view is 'an ugly thing', but it is not incompatible with 'distinction of style'; it is less important to warn the novice against it than to warn him against 'the curious superstition that the splitting or not splitting makes the difference between a good and a bad writer'. H. W. Fowler (1926) concludes his discussion with the view that splitting should not be gratuitously indulged in, but is preferable either to ambiguity (e.g. 'Our object is further to cement trade relations') or to artificiality (e.g. '. . . in not combining to forbid flatly hostilities'). However, as Logan Pearsall Smith (1925) records, 'the battle rages about the split infinitive, which horrifies the old-fashioned grammarian, but is more dispassionately regarded by linguists of the modern school'.

The American Leonard's historical survey (1929) largely confirmed that no mention of the split infinitive occurred in eighteenth-century authors, and concluded that 'it was both a discovery and an aversion of nineteenth-century grammarians'. His practical enquiry (1932) into twentieth-century views indicated that the pendulum seemed to have swung back again. Though authors and speech teachers found the split usage disputable, as a whole the group rated it 'established'; on this evidence, 'teachers who condemn it arbitrarily are wasting their time and that of their pupils'.

Opinions since the thirties have gone on fluctuating, with a tendency to crystallize round a compromise. Characteristic of many is the position of Treble and Vallins (1936); following Fowler, they advocate avoidance of splitting except when such avoidance would lead to 'stilted or self-conscious awkwardness or actual ambiguity'. Low and Hollingworth (1941) simply designate the split infinitive 'a common error of style', but Partridge (1947) recommends either avoidance (whenever possible) or bold use of it—adding somewhat cryptically that 'the angels are on our side'. Leacock (1944) suggests that 'many of our actual verbs are in themselves split infinitives, as when we say *to undertake* and *to overthrow*'. He defends deliberate splitting in characteristic fashion: 'Many of us who write books are quite willing to split an "infinitive" or to half split it or quite split it according to effect. We might even be willing to sometimes so completely, in order to gain a particular effect, split the infinitive as to practically but quite consciously run the risk of leaving the *to* as far behind as the last caboose of a broken freight train.' Lewis's (1949) example, 'We must remember *to accurately check* each answer', was voted acceptable only by 53 per cent of his judges, but some, he says, voted against this particular example rather than against the construction in general.

Hugh Sykes Davies (1951) has a short chapter on 'The Unsplittable Infinitive', in which he asserts that the *to* is not part of the infinitive but merely a preposition with no more right to strict contiguity with its verb than any other preposition has to what follows. In his view the

superstition that it has this right arose from the assumption that
English grammar depends on Latin, and that consequently *to love* is
as much a unity as the *amare* printed alongside it in textbooks. To
illustrate his advice on splitting or not according to the desired emphasis, he quotes from Harold Nicolson: 'It would be impossible, I
feel, to actually be as decadent as Lambert looked. I split the infinitive
deliberately, being in the first place no non-split diehard (oh, the
admirable Mr Fowler!), and desiring secondly to emphasize what
was in fact the dominant and immediate consideration which Lambert
evoked.' Vallins (1951) might have classed his contemporary Davies
with Fowler as one who protests too much, so that 'the anti-split-
infinitive campaign has been so successful that most writers nowadays...
will cheerfully commit the sin of ambiguity rather than risk the self-
appointed grammarian's frown'. Similarly, Gowers (1954) finds that
avoidance of splitting has become a bogy 'to such a devastating effect
that people are beginning to feel that it must be wrong to put an
adverb between any auxiliary and any part of a verb, or between any
preposition and any part of a verb', and that they must therefore
commit such unnatural phrasing as 'They appeared completely to have
adjusted themselves to it' or even 'we have succeeded entirely in
unweaving it'.

Recent pronouncements—e.g. West and Kimber (1957), Collins
(1960)—have briefly reiterated the compromise advice of avoidance
unless intelligibility is threatened. But a new angle on why to be
chary of splitting is that of the American R. A. Hall (1964); his view
is that splitting, though quite legitimate, should be used sparingly
because of the 'many emotional overtones of hostility and diffidence'
that have developed around it.

In our enquiry, the split infinitive item earned a middle position
(24th of 50) in the acceptability rating, with an overall average
acceptance of 40 per cent. This average concealed one of the wider
'spreads'—from 66 per cent acceptability in Informal Speech to 19
per cent in Formal Writing. The implication—a very arguable one—
is that it is a kind of colloquialism that can be avoided without loss by
more careful phrasing. The order of tolerance by occupational groups
varied little between situations, but differed from the norm for the
whole fifty usages in that teachers were more lenient than usual (in
fact, hardly less lenient than students), whereas non-educationists
were unusually hostile—even more so than examiners. Many of the
comments referred to the issue in general terms, but it is possible that—

as with Lewis—the particular item was, by some, judged in isolation and found to have no advantage over the more puristic 'He refused *even to think* of it'.

ITEM 31.   They would accept this if it *was* offered.

The particular issue here is whether the subjunctive form *were* should replace *was*. The *O.E.D.*, with citations ranging from 971 to 1878, identifies the criterion for choice of mood after *if* as the preparedness of the user to endorse the truth of the *if*-statement: 'The indicative after *if* implies that the speaker expresses no adverse opinion as to the truth of the statement in the clause; it is consistent with his acceptance of it . . . The subjunctive after *if* implies that the speaker guards himself from endorsing the truth or realization of the statement; it is consistent with his doubt of it.' In borderline cases, it is claimed, the indicative is preferred.

The more general question of the status of the subjunctive in English, not only after *if*, is discussed in some detail by Margaret Schlauch (1959). She traces the declining fortunes of the subjunctive mood from the fifteenth century, when it was 'still widely employed'. Thereafter it 'continued to be syntactically important throughout the Renaissance period. Usage required it in clauses following main verbs expressing doubt, contingency and conditions, as well as other clauses where modern English has simple indicative, now using special auxiliaries to convey the semantic distinction from factual statements.' Shakespeare, she points out, used either indicative or subjunctive in *if*-clauses expressing possibility—'If thou *art* privy to thy country's fate' (*Hamlet*) contrasts with 'If music *be* the food of love' (*Twelfth Night*)—but regularly used the subjunctive for conditions contrary to fact, as in 'If a man *were* porter of hell-gate' (*Macbeth*). A nice contrast is implied in Othello's 'I think my wife *be* honest and I think she *is* not . . .'.

From the first, distinguished writers had used the indicative where the subjunctive might have been expected. Marckwardt and Walcott (1938) and other authorities list examples from, among others, Marlowe, Pepys, Defoe, Sheridan, Jane Austen and Charlotte Brontë. Leonard (1929) documents in detail the growing gulf between theory and practice in the eighteenth century. Early grammarians of that period (e.g. Greenwood and Harris) found that English had no moods, but Dr Johnson supplied the deficiency by announcing a 'conjunctive mode'. His views were supported by Lowth, Priestley, Buchanan and others, though with various qualifications. Webster, after some wavering, claimed that, after *if*, both *were* and *was* were 'correct' hypothetical subjunctive forms. In fact, as Schlauch remarks, it was in such constructions that the subjunctive form persisted longest; elsewhere it was increasingly ousted by modal auxiliaries which took over the function of expressing doubt, contingency, possibility and the like.

The issue was by no means disposed of, of course. In 1877 a writer to *Notes and Queries* recalled 'the rule', which he had never seen reason to question, that 'Sentences which imply contingency and futurity require the subjunctive mood; but when contingency and futurity are not both implied the indicative ought to be used'. In the twentieth century the position has been very variously assessed. As early as 1901, Brander Matthews thought the English subjunctive obsolescent, so that 'posterity will not need to clog its memory with any rule for the employment of the subjunctive; and the English language will have cleansed itself of a barnacle.' The Fowlers (1906) dismissed *if I be* and *it were* as archaisms for which the 'modern prose English' equivalents are *if I am* and *it would be*. In the more detailed arguments of H. W. Fowler (1926), the singular *were* is seen as 'a recognizable subjunctive, and applicable not to past facts, but to present or future non-facts; it is entirely out of place in an *if*-clause concerned with past actualities and not answered by a *were* or *would be* in the apodosis'. Of the four classes distinguished by Fowler—alives, revivals, survivals and arrivals —our example seems to belong to the last, along with 'If it *were* (or nowadays alternatively *was*) so how angry we should be'.

The sentence used in Leonard's investigation (1932) was: 'If it *wasn't* for football, school life would be dull.' With a great majority of his judges approving this as 'good colloquial usage', it was ranked as 'established'. Fries (1940) found in his 'standard English' materials twelve instances of the conditional subjunctive but thirty-three of the indicative in exactly parallel conditions; he concluded that 'in general the subjunctive has tended to disappear from English'. Support for Fowler's discrimination between reference to past facts as against present or future non-facts may perhaps be found in the low 'acceptance ratio' of a non-fact clause used by Lewis (1949). Only 34 per cent of his judges tolerated 'She acts as if she *was* my wife', though it is only fair to add that reactions ranged widely, from the clear favourable majorities of professors, lexicographers and authors to the overwhelming rejection ('by a vociferous 12 to 1') by the editors of women's magazines. Against this background the assertion of Somerset Maugham, quoted by Vallins (1951), that American writers use the subjunctive much more than we do looks over-simple. Maugham, turning to the British scene, adds that 'the primness of language which teachers inculcate is forced upon them by the general slovenliness and incorrectness of speech common to their pupils. They are kicking against the pricks; the subjunctive mood is in its death throes, and the best thing to do is to put it out of its misery as soon as possible.'

Nevertheless, it is not being allowed to die unmourned on either side of the Atlantic. In England, Hornby (1954) advises foreigners that, though *was* is used as an alternative to *were* in *if*-clauses in spoken English, the subjunctive form *were* (with a singular subject) is usual in literary English in conditional clauses. Collins (1960) more positively defines the circumstances in which *if* should be followed by the subjunctive as: 'Where there is uncertainty, supposition or speculation; where the statement is imaginative, not factual; where a condition is improved [*sic*—imposed?].' Examining bodies, according to Halliday *et al.* (1964), seek to perpetuate an archaic subjunctive; a Scottish University Entrance examination, for instance, required treatment of 'grammatically incorrect' sentences that included 'If I was you, I should not go'. A recent American statement—Wilson Follett (1966) —concedes that 'the subjunctive mood has almost disappeared from English speech and is retreating, though more slowly, from written prose', but argues that in statements contrary to fact the use of the subjunctive still distinguishes educated from uneducated speech, as in 'If he *were* to move to California'.

Though our respondents were conspicuously tolerant of 'if it *was*' in Informal Speech (77 per cent acceptance), they were very much less so (21 per cent) at the other extreme, Formal Writing. This wide divergence (7th of the 50 in order of magnitude) kept the average acceptance down to 46 per cent, placing the usage 15th on the acceptability table. Sharp variations from the normal pattern of reaction by occupational groups were expressed in the unusual harshness of the non-educationists and the comparative leniency of the examiners, who constituted the least harsh group overall and in all situations except Formal Writing. (Even there, they were more tolerant than two other groups.)

ITEM 32. **He did it *quicker* than he had ever done it before.**
The acceptability of *quicker* as comparative adverb is linked to the acceptability of *quick* as the corresponding 'positive' or unmarked

6

form. The prevalence of adjective/adverb pairs distinguished by *-ly* has bred the popular assumption that no form can itself be an adverb if there exists an equivalent *-ly* adverb form. But there is plenty of evidence supporting an 'unmarked' adverb form; the *O.E.D.* gives examples from about 1330 to 1840 (Dickens).

Greenough and Kittredge (1902) include *quick* in their list of 'flat' adverbs; others are *slow* (see Item 53), *fast, cheap, still*, and *sound* ('to sleep *sound*'). They constitute 'an ancient and dignified part of our language'. Fowler (1926), in an article on the 'unidiomatic *-ly*', is less restrained: 'much more to be deprecated than all the particular departures from idiom already mentioned is the growing notion that every monosyllabic adjective, if an adverb is to be made of it, must have a *-ly* clapped on to it to proclaim the fact'. He points out, not only that there are many forms (e.g. *much*) where this is plainly not so, but also that with some it can invite misunderstanding. In particular he instances *hardly*, which if used to mean adverbial *hard*, may be read as *scarcely*. Context may rescue 'this *hardly* contested and essential point', but it won't help 'For attendance at the workhouse he receives £105 a year, which, under the circumstances, is *hardly* earned'. Partridge (1947) finds a stylistic distinction, the *-ly* forms being more polite, the root forms more vigorous, but vouchsafes no reason for this view. A possibly more reasonable observation is that of Hornby (1954), who suggests that *quick* is used colloquially as an adverb after common verbs of movement, but that elsewhere (e.g. Retribution *quickly* followed) the *-ly* form is used. Recent handbooks have not all agreed. Whereas Collins (1960), for instance, accepts locutions such as 'Do not walk *quick*', Golding (1964) finds the same usage wrong in 'He talks French too *quick* for me to understand him'. In a long article on 'adverbs, vexatious', Follett (1966) says nothing about *quick(ly)* as such, but strongly defends the unmarked adverb. He points out that we would not think of 'going *straightly* to the point', of 'being *widely* awake' or of 'coming too *lately*'. He deplores condemnation of the advertiser's slogan 'Dress *Right*—You Can't Afford Not To'; the allegedly grammatical *rightly* would be as odd as the reviewer's amendment of the title of Sholokhov's novel to 'And Quiet*ly* Flows the Don'. In any case, insistence on *-ly* for all adverbs will not eliminate adjectives in *-ly* such as *badly, likely, lovely, friendly, soldierly*.

Forty-two per cent of responses by our judges were favourable, placing this item just in the upper half (22nd) of the acceptability table. The 'spread' in acceptance between Informal Speech and Formal

Writing was one of the largest, but the order of tolerance among occupational groups was close to the average. One might wonder whether a more lenient view would have been taken of the root-form *quick* (e.g. The doctor came *quick*) than of *quicker*, but the evidence of Item 53 suggests not. Though presented only in the two informal situations, 'go *slow*' achieved a general acceptance (40 per cent) even less than that of Item 32.

ITEM 33. **He did not actually dislike football; he was just** *disinterested.*

The use of *disinterested* in the sense, not of *unbiased*, but of *not interested*, is often quoted—e.g. by Richards (1955)—as an example of the 'degradation of language'. A fairer comment is that of Follett (1966), who also regrets the confusion between *dis-* and *un-interested* that has developed, but realizes that the former word 'has swung back to an earlier meaning, after a period of valuable service in a post where at the moment no replacement is in sight'. The *O.E.D.* confirms this account; *disinterested* came first (before 1610), but in the sense of *not interested*, while *uninterested* arrived later (before 1646) in the sense of *impartial*. In the course of the seventeenth century each seems to have acquired the other's meaning in addition to its own; later, when the two terms were again disentangled, each preserved its acquired rather than its original sense.

The twentieth century seems to be producing another intermingling of the two words. As early as 1927 the American Krapp comments on the occasional *un-/dis-* confusion. In England, Treble and Vallins (1936) and Partridge (1947) protest against the same development. Vallins (1951) repeats the condemnation, adding that *disinterested* is an 'absolute' word which is never part of a prepositional phrase with *in* or *by*. Gowers (1954) illustrates misuse by the seeming paradox of a Minister of State (whose duty as a public figure is to be *disinterested*) claiming innocence of the charge of being *disinterested* in a certain matter. In the same year the American linguist Hill acknowledges regret at the blurring of a useful distinction and the consequently increased risk of misunderstanding, but insists that it is a less important thing than is sometimes suggested. The change is one small part of the swings-and-roundabouts process by which some items of vocabulary are lost and others gained; and in any case lexical form is less significant than grammatical structure.

The handbooks of the 1960s, however, still resist change. For Collins

(1960) it is wrong to use *dis-* for *un-interested*; Lieberman (1964) tersely condemns the practice and Berry (1963) thinks that those who follow it should know better. More tolerant is the linguist Barber (1964), who reminds us of the chequered history of the two words, thinks the current confusion between them an innovation rather than a return to seventeenth-century usage, and notes that the adjectival development has led to the revival of the noun *disinterest* for 'lack of interest'. 'Wise men', as Follett says (with more than a hint of irony), 'have declared that the battle over *disinterested* has been lost.' Certainly, distinguished men are among the 'offenders'; the head of a very famous public school, for instance, has written that most L.E.A.s were unenthusiastic about boarding education and 'Miss Wilkinson's successors were *disinterested*'.

Our own respondents were markedly hostile. With only 34 per cent acceptances, the usage came 32nd in the order of acceptability. The very narrow 'spread' between Informal Speech (39 per cent) and Formal Writing (29 per cent) doubtless reflected the view that a serious meaning-distinction was at stake, irrespective of the occasion and type of communication. In all situations, the occupational groups reacted characteristically. The students (54 per cent acceptances) were distinctly more permissive than any other group; the examiners (6 per cent) were extremely unsympathetic.

ITEM 34. **Reference will be made to the *historic* development of mathematics.**

The *O.E.D.* gives *historical* as one meaning of *historic*, with supporting examples from 1669 to 1871. But today (except for the special grammatical use in 'historic tenses') the two terms seem to live in amicable separation, with a clear demarcation of *historical* as meaning 'pertaining to history' from *historic* in the sense of 'notable or memorable'. The possibility of confusion is therefore not a very real one for most people.

Fowler (1926) finds the differentiation fairly complete in his day, so that 'the use of one in a sense now generally expressed by the other is a definite backsliding'. Most of the handful of more recent books that find the matter worth mention—e.g. Treble and Vallins (1936), Partridge (1947), Collins (1960)—confine themselves to recording the difference in usage. That Follett (1966) includes a whole paragraph about it implies that blurring of the distinction does occur, at least in the U.S.A., but he does not explicitly complain. He asserts firmly that '*historic* = special; *historical* = actual'; everything *historic* is in a sense *historical*, but not vice versa.

Our choice of example was perhaps less than happy at a time when sensational developments in the 'new mathematics' might conceivably be thought *historic* in the sense of deserving a place in *historical* record. Consequently the figure of 29 per cent acceptance might be inflated and the position of the item (38th of 50) on the acceptability table rather higher than it deserves. This complication would not, however, explain why students and non-educationists, with 42 per cent and 35 per cent acceptances, were conspicuously more tolerant than the other groups.

ITEM 35. **Neither author nor publisher *are* subject to censorship.**

The point here is subject-verb concord. Is a plural verb acceptable with a 'disjunctive' subject of which both parts are singular? Both the alleged offence and condemnation of it have long histories. The *O.E.D.* cites examples of the plural usage from Shakespeare, Dryden, Johnson, Ruskin and other famous writers of the past.

Denunciation of a simple *neither* with plural verb certainly goes back to the eighteenth century—for instance, to Knowles (4th edition 1796), who lists 'Neither of these *are* mine' and 'Neither of us *deny* . . .' among 'Improper Expressions'. A century later White (1870) was insisting that *either* and *neither* are essentially separative and thereby cannot take plural verbs. But at the same period a writer to *Notes and Queries* (1877)—already quoted in connection with Item 12— admitted, albeit with regret, that the use of *neither* for any number and with a plural verb had become normal practice; in his view, a sentence such as 'Three amendments were proposed, but *neither* of them *were* carried' would be 'ordinary newspaper statement'. A less startling departure from orthodoxy—'Neither of the two men *are* convicts'— is allowed by Krapp (1927) to have 'a natural if not a correct grammatical ring', because of 'the predominantly plural character of the whole thought'. The American attitude was investigated by Leonard (1932), who included in his test both a simple *neither . . . are* sentence and the *neither . . . nor . . . are* sentence which we borrowed from him. Both usages were rated 'disputable'. The author-publisher one was more readily received by linguists than by others; greatest opposition came from the authors, who 'were almost unanimous in condemning the expression as illiterate'—a reaction perhaps all the more surprising in that the 'illiteracy' had been taken from Galsworthy. The uncertainty of status of this usage in America is further illustrated by the contrast between the observations of Fries (1940), who found the plural verb commonly used with *neither* by his Group II speakers (representing 'the great mass of the people in most of our communities') and the recent opinion of Follett (1966) that such usage occurs only occasionally—'all aberrations being possible'.

In England, the Fowlers (1906) tersely commented on the marked neglect—e.g. by Jowett, Thackeray and Trollope—of the 'rule' that '*neither, either*, as pronouns, should always take a singular verb'. Twenty years later, H. W. Fowler (1926) was only slightly less rigorous. He still made no concessions to the great—'The right course is not to indulge in bad grammar ourselves and then plead that better men like Johnson and Ruskin have done it before us, but to follow what is the accepted as well as the logical rule'—but admitted that difficulties could arise (e.g. 'Neither you nor I *is? am? are?*') which could only satisfactorily be met by complete rephrasing. Partridge (1947) similarly asserted that the plural construction was an error, even though the experts committing the error included the great Dean Alford. Gowers (1954) describes 'the common attraction of the verb into the plural when the subject is *either* or *neither*' as a blunder—though 'in one or two exceptional instances the force of this attraction has conquered the grammarians'. The handbooks—e.g. Barclay, Knox and Ballantyne (1945), Collins (1960), Golding (1964)—tend merely to demand the singular verb.

In our enquiry, this item—with only 31 per cent acceptance—came well down in the order of acceptability (34th of 50). Only the students, and they only in Informal Speech, gave it a majority vote. The examiners, with 11 per cent acceptance, were by far the least sympathetic group. The possibility that our direct mode of presentation, by putting judges on their mettle, encouraged undue censoriousness seems the more plausible by reason of the contrast between our results and those obtained a year or so later by Quirk and Svartvik (1966), using a different and indirect technique. In their test of 'linguistic acceptability', they required respondents to make choices involved in converting items from one pattern, tense, number, etc., to another. The test included several *neither . . . nor* items. For purposes of comparison the most relevant items were those in which past tense was to be replaced by present in 'Neither he nor I knew the answer' and 'Neither I nor he felt a thing'. Disregarding the complication of varied subject-order (the order 'I nor he' caused some discomfort), the investigators found a preference for the unmarked form (i.e. the plurals *know, feel*) in the ratio 2:1.

ITEM 36. *One* **rarely likes to do as** *he* **is told.**
Is it permissible for the specific pronoun *he* to be used to refer back to an antecedent unspecific *one*? Strict grammatical consistency demands '*one . . . one*', but this construction—especially if prolonged (as in Follett's example: '*One* is entitled to do as *one* likes as long as *one* does not trample on *one's* obligations to *one's* fellows')—is intolerably stilted and laborious. On the whole, Americans tend to sacrifice grammatical rigour to naturalness, whereas the British adhere more doggedly to the 'rule'. In this sense, the label 'Americanism' is justified for our item, but it does not alter the fact that the 'inconsistent' usage (one . . . he/his/they, etc.) has a very long pedigree. The *O.E.D.*'s citations start as far back as 1477, with '. . . *one* was surer in keeping *his* tunge, than in moche spekyng'.

Demands for strict consistency go back in this country at least as far as Dean Alford (1869), who insisted that *one* be followed by *one's* and *oneself*, never by *he, his, they*, etc. For breaches of his rule, he partly blames the influence of French usages such as 'Avec cette sauce *on* pourrait manger *son* père'. But it seems unlikely that this factor swayed scholars of the time who used '*one . . . his*' quite naturally—for example, the two editors of scholarly works on education who wrote respectively 'The slower *one* goes over the book, the faster grows *his* original power of thinking' (Harris, 1887) and 'To be abused tries *one's* temper, but need not diminish *his* self-esteem' (Keatinge, 1896). In the twentieth century, Fowler (1926) accepts divergence between practice and theory, but advocates that the former should give way to the latter; in his view the modern idiom of '*one . . . one*' has such advantages that 'it should be made universal'. Not very impressively, he points out that it makes possible a differentiation between the numeral *one* (e.g. *One* hates *his* enemies and another forgives them) and the impersonal one (e.g. *One* hates *one's* enemies . . .); it also obviates 'recourse to the horrible *their* (*One* does not like to have *their* word doubted)'. Treble and Vallins (1936) and Low and Hollingworth (1941) dislike 'inconsistency', but Partridge (1947) rather surprisingly concedes that '*one* is made to feel that *he* must trust himself' is strictly correct, however awkwardly it reads. Gowers (1954) counsels avoidance of the dilemma: 'Any sentence that needs to repeat the impersonal *one* is bound to be inelegant, and you will do better to rewrite it.' Recent handbooks (West and Kimber, 1957; Berry, 1963; Golding, 1964) have tried to revive the strict 'consistency' rule.

In America, Krapp (1927) favours the rule in principle, but recommends rephrasing to avoid a 'stylistically stilted' series of *one's*. Leonard (1932) gives similar advice, even though his judges in general were sufficiently lenient towards '*one . . . he*' (in the same sentence as ours) for it to be counted as 'established'. On the other hand, Perrin (1939) is quoted as favouring the mixed construction—'American usage stands firmly by older English usage in referring back to *one* by *he, his, him* (or *she, her*)'—and the quoter (Kennedy, 1942) himself admits to 'a personal preference for this non-British usage'. The most recent American pronouncement, by Follett (1966), is also the most conservative. Though he sympathizes with the motive of avoiding a sequence of *one's*, he finds that 'the reason is good, the solution not'. Not very convincingly, he finds possible ambiguity in such sentences as 'The criticisms are sweepingly extravagant, but *one* senses also that *he* must not dismiss them entirely', and accordingly asserts that 'when the pronoun *one* stands for anyone at all, it should not serve as the antecedent of *he*'.

Our respondents were distinctly intolerant of our item; with an overall average acceptability of only 20 per cent, it came very low (44th) in the table of acceptance. Even in Informal Speech it failed to muster a 50 per cent approval (only 42 per cent of the students tolerated it).

ITEM 37. **Roller-skating is very different *to* ice-skating.**
The choice we are primarily concerned with here is that between *to* and *from*. (The legitimacy of the other claimant, *than*, is discussed mainly under Item 23.) The objection usually made against *to* is that it contradicts the etymological force of the *dis-* prefix constituting the first syllable of *different*; since this prefix indicates separation or disjunction, the appropriate particle, it is argued, is *from*. Furthermore, this construction would be consistent with the normal verbal form 'to differ *from*'.

The *O.E.D.* records that the usual construction is now the one with *from*; the *to* construction 'is found in writers of all ages, and is frequent colloquially, but is by many considered incorrect'. Examples of the latter, dating from 1526, are found in Dekker, Fielding and Thackeray.

The list is extended by Webster (1920) to include Jane Austen ('How different *to* your brother and mine').

Perhaps inevitably, the *to* usage came under attack in the eighteenth century. Leonard quotes from Baker (1770) the opinion that, though 'often used by good writers', it is 'exceptionable'. 'Is not the word *From* here more natural than *To*?' asks Baker, 'and does it not make better Sense?' A century later Alford (1869) found the *to* construction 'entirely against all reason and analogy', and he attempts to clinch the argument by asserting that *different* is only a participle of the verb to *differ*.

It appears that Americans do not have this problem. Among those placing *different to* firmly in British English are: Fitzedward Hall (1873), who described it as 'essentially an English colloquialism' and explained it as motivated by an instinct of euphony rather than of scientific analogy; White (1899), who observes that 'it pervades British speech and literature even of the highest class'; Brander Matthews (1901), who categorizes it as a 'Briticism'; Webster (1920), who finds it a peculiarly British usage, especially in colloquial speech; Krapp (1927), who more tentatively thinks it an alternative in England to the commoner *from* construction; and Follett (1966), who rates *different to* as almost non-existent in the U.S.A., while it and *different from* share 'prevailing British written usage'.

In England, the judgement of the Fowlers in 1906 was that the *to* usage was undoubtedly gaining ground and would probably displace *from* 'in no long time'; meanwhile, it was advisable to avoid it and the disapproval it attracted. Some confirmation of the prophecy is found in H. W. Fowler; in 1926 he found objections to *different to* (and incidentally to *averse to*, etc.) 'mere pedantries'. He also despatched the 'hasty and ill-defined generalization' that adjectives or participles should 'conform to the construction of their parent verbs'. Partridge (1947) retorts to the allegations of 'Briticism' by observing that 'different *than*' was becoming increasingly frequent in the American press. Gowers (1951) mentions all three particles, recognizing good authority for *to*, but regarding *from* as established usage and *than* as carelessness. He subsequently (1954) noted—as we mentioned in discussing Item 23—that *different than* is 'not unknown even in *The Times*'. Vallins (1951) contrasts *different from* with *indifferent to*. The stiffening of attitude in some recent handbooks is exemplified by the stern pronouncement of Golding (1964) that 'English idiom demands that particular words should be followed by particular prepositions'.

Our *different to* usage did not commend itself much to our judges. Students and non-educationists cast over 60 per cent of Informal Speech votes in its favour, but elsewhere minority approval prevailed. The overall acceptance rate averaged out at 30 per cent, placing the item well down (35th of 50) in the table of acceptability.

ITEM 38.   ***These sort of plays* need first-class acting.**

The question here is whether the collective plural sense of the italicized cluster may be allowed to over-ride the strict grammatical need for a singular deictic *this* (and, incidentally, a singular verb *needs*) to preserve concord with *sort*. That the plural 'feeling' has often prevailed is witnessed by the *O.E.D.*'s citation of instances of *these/those sort of* from 1551. Shakespeare contributes several (e.g. '*these kind* of knaves' in *Lear*, '*these* set *kind* of fools' in *Twelfth Night*), and Pope, Swift, Addison and Trollope are among those who have not hesitated to use it. Defenders of concord have as reserve alternative the construction 'plays of this sort'.

Alford (1869) sets out the problem with admirable clarity: 'It is evident that this tendency to draw the less important word into similarity to the more important one, is suffered to prevail over strict grammatical exactness.' He contrasts this pull with the opposing tendency in 'this kind of thing' or 'that sort of thing', where logically the sense demands *things*. A correspondent to *Notes and Queries* (1877) found this last proposal (as in 'This kind of things is so pretty') just as objectionable as the 'mixed' formula of 'These kind of . . .'

The dispute has persisted into the twentieth century. The Fowlers (1906) included *these sort of*, as used by Trollope and Marie Corelli, in a set of 'Vulgarisms and Colloquialisms'. Presumably this classifies the brothers with those grammarians who, according to Logan Pearsall Smith (1925), had succeeded in 'stigmatizing as a vulgarism' an idiom which was once correct, which figured in the usage of good authors, and which was at least as acceptable as 'by *this* means'. Meanwhile, however, H. W. Fowler (1926) had relaxed his objections to the extent of accepting *these sort of* as 'irregular but idiomatic', and finding it and the like usages as easy to forgive (at least in party talk) as they are to avoid.

Treble and Vallins (1936) contrast 'These sort of things interest me' (definitely ungrammatical) with 'This sort of things interests me' (awkward and unidiomatic, but at least grammatical) and with 'This sort of thing interests me' (grammatical and idiomatic). They strongly favour the third pattern, though they seem to sympathize with Alford's doubt about its logicality by offering as alternative 'Things of this sort'. Gowers (1954) includes the 'mixed' construction among his shibboleths and from *Punch* quotes a little poem beginning:

Did you say those sort of things
Never seem to you to matter?
Gloomily the poet sings
Did you say those sort of things?

He adds that, though 'we have a better sense of values today', it is as well to humour the purists by writing 'things of that kind'. Recent handbooks are more tersely prescriptive. Collins (1960) wants 'those sort of' replaced by 'of that sort' or 'that sort of'; Lieberman (1964) condemns 'I like *these kind* of shoes' and approves 'I like *this kind* of shoes'; and Golding (1964) labels a similar pair 'wrong' and 'correct' respectively.

In America, Krapp (1927) admitted that *these sort* can be defended on grounds of reason, though such defence could not make it unquestioned good grammatical English. Leonard (1929) thought that '*This kind* of men are' was accepted in standard English, while *these kind* and *those sort* were 'reputed uncultivated, at least in the United States'. Confirmation of the latter's unacceptability was supplied by the editors who answered his questionnaire (1932); they unanimously placed 'Don't get *these kind* of gloves' at the very bottom of their list. The linguists, however, ranked it higher than the other groups, and the resultant classification was 'disputable'. Somewhat unexpectedly, instances of *these/those* with *kind of/sort of* were found by Fries (1940) in his Standard English correspondence, but not in the Vulgar English material.

Our respondents were on the whole not disposed to accept the usage at all readily. With only 29 per cent acceptances, it ranked 37th of the fifty items. Students, though twice as lenient as any other group, averaged only 45 per cent approval. The 'spread' between Informal Speech and Formal Writing was about average, but—with groups separately and together—the widest gap was between Informal Speech (53 per cent general acceptability) and Informal Writing (33 per cent). It is interesting to note that of our 457 respondents fewer than sixty claimed to accept in Formal Writing a construction authorized in the works of Shakespeare and other 'classic' writers of English.

ITEM 39. **You will learn that *at university*.**

The propriety of omitting *the* before *university* (and some similar nouns) is slightly complicated by an associated choice between *at* and *in*. On the latter aspect, the *O.E.D.* records that *at*, by contrast with *in* or *on*, is sometimes used to express some practical connexion with a place, rather than mere local position. It instances pairs such as *in school/at school, in/on the sea, in prison/at the hotel*. (The last of these is the least convincing; it could be argued that a prisoner's connexion with his gaol is more practical than local, while the reverse might be true of a hotel-guest.) Other examples of *at* phrases, over a very long period (1000 to 1840) illustrate the frequent omission of the article—e.g. at home, at church, at college, at court.

The paucity of comment on this usage indicates that the issue is far from pressing—perhaps because only in recent years has the tendency to omit the article extended beyond a few familiar phrases. Barber (1964) illustrates the omitting of *the* before independent noun-phrases (e.g. 'the necessity for raising Bank Rate'; *Radio Times*) as well as in prepositional phrases (e.g. in U.S.A.). He includes *university* (with *government, temperature, theatre,* etc.) in a list of nouns before which *the* may be dropped in any situation. In a BBC broadcast (May 1965) Simeon Potter similarly noted this development, as in 'going to university'. It may well be that press and radio journalism, with an emphasis on compression and slickness, exercises strong influence in this direction. Anthony Crosland, for instance, has been reported as finding a proposal for a Royal Commission 'a matter solely for government' (*Education*, November 1965).

Our respondents encouraged the view that there is no great objection to this usage. An average acceptance rate of 67 per cent placed the item near the top (6th) of the acceptability table. It was, in fact, one of the half-dozen usages supported in all situations to the extent of over half the total responses. Students were well-disposed towards it (78 per cent tolerance) and teachers (67 per cent) for once more so than lecturers and non-educationists. On the other hand, more than half the examiners' total votes were cast against it, with acceptance ranging from 69 per cent in Informal Speech to 26 per cent in Formal Writing.

ITEM 40. ***Pulling the trigger*, the gun went off unexpectedly.**

The italicized item includes, in *pulling*, what has been variously stigmatized as an unrelated, misrelated, unattached, isolated, disconnected, suspended, hanging, or dangling participle. By many it is deemed to infringe the Law of Proximity, according to which a participle should be placed close to the subject of its root-verb (above, the 'puller' of the trigger), lest otherwise it attach itself to a nearby but inappropriate alternative (here, 'the gun'). The alleged misuse has been found in many respectable writers. According to Pooley (1946), J. Lesslie Hall (1917) listed from his own reading 189 instances of the isolated participle or gerund in 68 authorities from Latimer to Stevenson and concluded that: 'The "misrelated participle" goes back to the Anglo-Saxon period. It is found both in prose and in poetry. It comes out clearly in Mandeville and Chaucer . . . It is seen in the Mystery Plays, Latimer, Shakespeare, and in every decade down to the present day. It is used in polite society and by cultivated speakers without number. Certainly it may be called the "misapprehended", the "persecuted" participle.' But Fowler (1926) sternly warns us that this evidence is no extenuation, for 'it is now not a sufficient defence for looseness of this kind to produce parallels, as can very easily be done, even from great writers of past generations'.

As might be expected, the issue is not as simple as it is sometimes represented to be. The Fowlers (1906) disapproved of all 'unattached or wrongly attached' participles, but conceded that 'there are degrees of heinousness in the offence'. Their examples of eight such degrees ranged from 'participles that have passed into prepositions, conjunctions, or members of adverbial phrases' (e.g. *Considering* the circumstances, you may go)—and are therefore incorrect only if rated still as participles—to 'really bad' instances such as Charlotte Brontë's '*Being pushed* unceremoniously to one side . . . he usurped my place'. H. W. Fowler advocated the fighting of a delaying action. He argued that a clear acknowledgement of the legitimacy of the usage where prepositional or adverbial status had been conceded by all but pedants 'should strengthen rather than weaken the necessary protest against the slovenly uses now to be illustrated', i.e. uses where such status had not been achieved.

Many other writers on the topic are briefer and less discriminating than this. Low and Hollingworth (1941) insist that the logical subject of a participle must not differ from that of the finite verb. Barclay, Knox and Ballantyne (1945) say that a participle should qualify the subject of the nearest finite verb. Vallins (1953) emphasizes the distinction between *mis*related forms, which tend to attach themselves to the 'wrong' noun, and *un*related or 'hanging' ones, which relate to an impersonal or 'dummy' *it* (e.g. *Knowing* how their promise was fulfilled, *it* is impossible to discover . . .) and dislikes both constructions. Gowers (1954), Collins (1960) and Golding (1964) merely illustrate the error.

The issue seems to have attracted less attention in America, but Follett (1966) has recently written at length about it. As hinted in the title of his article—'Danglers, Acceptable'—he is concerned with drawing a line between tolerable and intolerable instances. He sets the prepositional 'considering' construction (as in the Fowler example above) against a still participial construction in *'Considering* his situation likely to go from bad to worse, *he* decided to offer his resignation'. In his view, *according, concerning* and *owing (to)* have been 'completely transformed' from participle to preposition, but forms like *assuming* and certainly *looking* ('Looking seaward . . . eleven lighthouses are in view') remain true participles. The dubious intermediate zone accommodates not only *considering* but *admitting, defending, granting, providing, regarding, (broadly) speaking,* etc. Choice in these doubtful cases might be helped by the observation that 'a majority of the converted participles denote some kind of mental sensory activity; they are from verbs of thinking or perceiving'.

This discrimination operates to the disadvantage of our 'physical' act of 'pulling the trigger'. The responses of our judges supported this adverse view. With only 17 per cent acceptances, our item came near the bottom (46th of 50) of the table of acceptability. In terms of occupational groups, the order of tolerance varied from the average solely (but interestingly) in that non-educationists were more lenient even than students. This suggests the possibility that there was a touch of school pedantry in the general hostility of the four education-oriented groups.

ITEM 41. **He could write *as well or better than* most people.**
This is an example of what Fowler (1926) called 'unequal yokefellows'; failure to harness together two symmetrical items (as well *as*/better *than*) inflicts a 'passing discomfort on fastidious readers'. He admits that the offence does not seriously obstruct understanding, but thinks that the well-trained scrupulous writer does not commit it.

Leonard (1932) submitted almost the same sentence—'He could write *as well* or *better than* I'—to his panel. A reception with between 25 per cent and 75 per cent acceptance ranked it among his 'disputable' items, but more than half the judges tolerated it. While it is therefore impossible to condemn the usage as illiterate, Leonard thinks it awkward and hence to be avoided. In England, Vallins (1951) plausibly suggests that failure to complete the parallel construction in, for example, 'He is as tall and broader than I am' arises from the 'false economy' of dispensing with the second preposition or conjunction; the latter should be restored. Gowers (1954) more leniently finds it natural, and certainly no great crime, to say 'as good or better than ever'; to meet purist objections without becoming stilted he recommends the alternative 'as good as ever or better'. Collins (1960) makes the same point, but Berry (1963) and Golding (1964) merely insist on the second particle. Most recently, the American Follett (1966) also argues that 'the quickest extrication is to pick the two formulas apart and handle them separately', but points out that this device does not always work. Only a more drastic overhaul will rectify 'some students . . . had received equal or better marks than . . .'—for instance, 'received marks as good as . . . , if not better than' or—more economically— 'received marks equal or superior to . . .'.

Though our respondents were fairly tolerant of the omission in Informal Speech (64 per cent acceptance), they were much less so elsewhere. The overall 38 per cent acceptance placed the item half-way down the list (26th). A substantial minority of each group except the examiners were moderately well-disposed, but whereas in Informal Speech fifteen of the thirty-five examiners were tolerant, hardly any of them extended this attitude to other situations.

ITEM 42.   **She told Charles and *I* the whole story.**
The choice of *I* where grammar is thought to demand the objective form *me* occurs because of the frequency of collocations such as 'Charles and I' in subject-positions, where the *I* form is, of course, 'correct'. The severest critics of the 'misuse', which is by no means uncommon and seems to become commoner, sometimes—as Gowers (1954) remarks—blame school teachers of English for it. They say that the latter so ferociously attack combinations such as 'you and *me*' in certain circumstances that pupils infer that this formula is ungrammatical in all circumstances. This theory of 'over-correction' may help to explain the spread of the 'x and *I*' expression to inappropriate situations, but it can hardly be the whole story. It cannot account for the use of this pattern centuries ago—for 'To give you and *I* a right understanding' (1649) or 'Leave your Lady and *I* alone' (1710). (To these *O.E.D.* citations we could add Shakespeare's 'All debts are

cleared between you and *I*'—a prepositional construction to be considered under Item 55.)

On the general issue of case-distinctions in English, Fowler (1926)
concedes the possibility that our remaining case-forms may be doomed
to extinction and admits that 'there is behind them no essential
notion or instinct of case itself', but he refuses to support a policy
of letting the memory of case 'fade away as soon as we can agree
whether *I* or *me*, *she* or *her*, *who* or *whom*, is to be the survivor of the
pair'. He affirms his faith 'that case visible and invisible is an essential
part of the English language, and that the right policy is not to welcome neglect of its rules, but to demand that in the novels and the
newspapers, from which most of us imbibe our standards of language,
they should be observed'. Subsequent writers have tended to accept
this view, though—like Fowler—they offer no suggestions how acceptance of rules could be imposed upon novelists and journalists. Among
those who re-affirm the rule that objects of verbs must always be in the
objective case are Gorrell and Laird (1953), Gowers (1954), Pooley
(1960), Berry (1963), Lieberman (1964), and Golding (1964).

Our respondents, as expected, were not favourably disposed to our
item. With a mere 27 per cent acceptance-rate, it came well down the
acceptability list (40th of 50). The order of tolerance by occupational
groups corresponded to the average pattern, but with wider differentiation. The student group was conspicuously more lenient (nearly
twice so) than the next most favourable group (non-educationists),
and the latter much more so than the rest. In so far as an age-factor
might be involved, the indications would be of a further decline in
the already somewhat vestigial character of case in English.

ITEM 43. **It was *us* who had been singing.**

Is the objective-case pronoun (e.g. *us*) acceptable after *to be*, which—
according to traditional grammar—should be followed by a 'subject
complement' in the subjective or nominative case (e.g. *we*)? Some
modern 'structural' grammarians would argue that, since in English
word-order is a more significant grammatical device than case, and
since word-order favours a pre-verbal nominative but a post-verbal
accusative, forms like *us* (or *me* in 'It is *me*') are grammatically at least
as defensible as the nominatives favoured by the analogy of Latin.
While the more theoretically minded accept a general principle
applicable to all instances of the kind, more pragmatic judges differen-

tiate between particular usages. Some who accept the very common
'It's *me*' react against the parallel but rarer 'It's *us*'; others who accept
both when self-contained (e.g. in answer to the question 'Who's
there?') reject them when followed—as in our example—by a clause.
Of the multitude of commentators on the topic—and few writers
about usage ignore this item—many concentrate on 'It is *I/me*' without
clearly indicating whether they consider this locution a special problem
or an exemplar of a whole set of structures of the type. We shall try
and focus more particularly on the specific 'It was *us* who . . .' sample,
but cannot hope to exclude altogether the broader issue of word-order
versus case-form.

The *O.E.D.* describes the *us* construction as 'common in dialect
and colloquial use, and occasionally employed in writing'. It quotes
from Stevenson 'It's *us* must break the treaty . . .', and from William
James, 'Our bodies themselves, are they simply ours, or are they *us*?,
The dispute, however, goes a good deal further back. Alford (1869)
speculates on whether in fact the nominative usage (e.g. It is *I*) is not
an innovation of grammarians. In support of this possibility he adduces
Latham's contention that *me*, for instance, is not a real but only an
adopted accusative form, and that 'It is *I*' is 'a modernism, or rather a
grammaticism, introduced solely on some grammatical hypothesis'.
He also invokes the analogy of the Danish dative after *to be* (e.g. Det
er *os*=It is *us*). Alford concludes that 'It will be curious if, after all,
it should be proved that our much-abused colloquial phrase is the
really good English, and its rival a mistaken purism'. We cannot but
agree, though the oddity would not be unique in the strange world
of disputed usage. The force of Alford's analogy with Danish is weak-
ened, however, by the apparent fact that the Danish equivalent construction was itself rejected by some grammarians of the period.
Jespersen (1925) quotes from H. P. Selmer (1861) a description of
det er mig (it is *me*) as 'an unmistakable and gross grammatical mistake'.
Selmer, with a dogmatism remarkable even for grammarians of the
time, added that 'according to all laws, human and divine, it ought
of course to be *det er jeg* (it is *I*) . . . it is nothing else than the grossest
sin against the first and simplest and most incontrovertible laws of
thought and of grammar when in the case under discussion we employ
mig . . . for *jeg*'. This pronouncement justly earned from Jespersen the
comment that 'There is nothing whatever in logic which obliges
the predicative to stand in the same case as the subject, that is, in the
nominative. On the contrary the predicative is different from the

7

subject, and in many languages, Russian and Finnish for example, it stands (at any rate very commonly) in other cases such as the instrumental, the partitive, the essive or the translative. Accordingly "all laws divine and human" and "the most incontrovertible laws of thought" amount to nothing more than a rule of Latin grammar!' This Danish rebuke had in the English context been anticipated by Sweet (1876) who, in advance of his age in this as in other linguistic matters, also attacked 'ignorant grammarians' whose influence alone prevented such phrases as *it is me* from being adopted into the written language and acknowledged in the grammars.

The American Sapir (1921), emphasizing the grammatical power of word-order, confidently forecast that '*It is I* will one day be as impossible in English as *c'est je*, for *c'est moi*, is now in French'. (He could hardly have been expected to foresee that in 1968 it would be reported that extremist French students, extending their protests against the established order to linguistic territory, had adopted the slogan 'L'anarchie c'est je'!) The analogy with French is in any case not wholly convincing; a century and a half before Sapir, George Campbell (1776) had argued that the oblique cases of these French personal pronouns were 'indefinite forms usable as either nominative or accusative, that English has no corresponding forms, and that therefore no French parallel could be used in defence of 'these vulgar, but unauthorized idioms, *it is me, it is him*'. Leonard (1932), in his investigation of American practice, used four items involving a *to be* form followed by a personal pronoun. The one with a nominative pronoun (It was *I* that . . .) was treated as clearly 'established', while the other three, with objective case-forms (It is *me*. If it had been *us* . . . I'll swear that was *him*), were all rated 'disputable' by the judging-panel as a whole. The linguists, however, included all but the fourth example in their 'established' category.

Partridge (1947) declines to generalize; he points out that educated speakers who say 'It is *me*' would not say 'It's *him*' or 'It's *us*', nor even 'It is *me*' if that were followed by 'who wrote that essay'. Potter (1950) quotes utterances where the nominative form is unthinkable—Shelley's 'Be thou *me*, impetuous one!' and the familiar 'Fare *thee* well'. Among the various anecdotes illustrating the contention that 'It is *I*' is used only by grammarians and foreigners is one told by R. A. Hall (1950) about a certain 'very puristic' lady teacher, whom he calls Miss Fidditch. Her lesson on the importance of avoiding 'it's *me*', in obedience to the inflexible rule of grammar that the verb *to be* never takes a direct object, is interrupted by a knock on the door and the Principal's voice asking 'Who's there?' The teacher unhesitatingly replies: 'It's *me*—Miss Fidditch.' Similarly, according to Gorrell and Laird (1953), legend has it that the great American linguist George Lyman Kittredge was working late in his office one night when a suspicious student janitor demanded 'Who's in there?' The professor answered: 'It's all right. It's *me*, Kittredge.' 'The devil it is', retorted the student, 'Kittredge'd say "It is *I*".'

Most recent writers—e.g. Gowers (1954), West and Kimber (1957), Collins (1960)—stress the difference between colloquial speech, where 'It is *me*' is natural and 'It is *I*' stilted, and writing, where the reverse choice is preferable. Collins (1960), however, specifically condemns 'It is *us* who bought the house', even in speech. Berry (1963) dogmatically asserts the 'rule' requiring a predicative nominative. On the other hand, Halliday *et al.* (1964) insist that 'The attempt to justify *It is I* on linguistic grounds rests on a straightforward misunderstanding of English clause structure'.

The concentration of so many commentators on the shortest locution ('It is *I/me*') oversimplifies the issue. One of our respondents reported that he would be much less irritated by 'It was *us* he blamed'. Here the accusative *us* may feel in some way supported by an elliptical 'whom' postulated by some grammarians. Formal grammar does not justify this 'feel', since theoretically the case of a pronoun is determined by its relation to the preceding verb, but the influence of the following construction has misled eminent grammarians of the past. Leonard quotes the praise bestowed ironically by Baker (1770) on the 'extraordinary correctness' of 'inferior Writers' who wrote 'It was not *him* they attacked, *us* they slandered'. Similarly deceived by the 'backwash' from the following verb was Campbell (1776), when he defended 'It is not *me* you are in love with' on the ground that *me* is governed by *with*.

It may well be that a following *whom* rather than *who* clause (or, of course, the absence of any sequel) would have produced a more favourable response from our judges. With a mere 25 per cent acceptance and a fair 'spread' between Informal Speech and Formal Writing, the item came far down the acceptability-table (41st of 50). The only marked divergence from the standard pattern of group reactions was the unusually harsh attitude of the non-educationists, who averaged only 13 per cent acceptance, by contrast with the 18 per cent of the normally much stricter group of examiners.

ITEM 44. **Nowadays Sunday is not observed *like* it used to be.**
Is *like* an acceptable alternative to *as* in the conjunctive function of
introducing a clause of comparison? According to Follett (1966) it
was once but is no longer: 'The status of *like* is a topic of historical
linguistics, not a problem of usage. Linguists know that *like* was used
as a conjunction in the formative stages of the language and that it
was freely used so by writers before and for a long time after William
Langland, in the fourteenth century. Isolated recurrences of it have
turned up in the writing of standard authors during the last century
and a half, though there is no standard author who has used it
habitually.' Presumably in his view the *O.E.D.*'s earlier quotations—
e.g. from Lord Berners and Shakespeare—illustrate the legitimate use,
whereas those from later authors—e.g. Darwin and Morris—represent
isolated aberrations. The latter category would also include Dickens's
remark, in a letter to Forster about the death of Little Nell, that
'Nobody will miss her *like* I shall'. Follett admits that the usage is
common today—in written English, in spoken American, in advertising
copy—but insists that, 'because in workmanlike modern writing there
is no such conjunction', these are instances of *like* 'masquerading as a
conjunction'. In support of his argument, he interprets examples of
'the opposite error of substituting *as* in comparisons between substantives' (e.g. 'he was baffled, beaten—*as I*' instead of '. . . *like me*') as
evidence of 'an instinctive or acquired revulsion' from the misuse of
like as a conjunction. There is no doubt that some writers and speakers
are inhibited by uncertainties about *like* and *as*, but many more
than Follett seem prepared to recognize use *like* as a conjunction
without hesitation or sense of guilt. The subjective evidence of ears
and eyes suggests that Leacock (1944) may well be right in putting
the opposite viewpoint—that, despite the textbook bans, most people,
and 'even grammarians on a vacation' use *like* as a conjunction, and
'so do the best authors'. (He goes further and suggests that in fact
like is stronger than *as* in this function.) This trend is reflected in
Webster's Dictionary; whereas the second edition labels the conjunctive *like* 'illiterate' and 'incorrect', the third edition (admittedly a
controversial publication) accepts it as standard.

The whole issue is somewhat complicated by variations between
putative—and doubtless actual—usage on opposite sides of the Atlantic,
with American and British writers each attributing laxity to the other.
In 1901 Brander Matthews described the conjunctive *like* as a Briticism
that was 'very prevalent, not merely among the uneducated, but

among the more highly cultivated'. Fifty years later some English observers condemned it as an Americanism; Vallins (1951, 1953), for instance, not only found the alleged Americanism to be gaining ground in modern usage, but even attributed Churchill's use of it in 'We are overrun by them [*sc.* by special committees], *like* the Australians were by rabbits' to his transatlantic family connexions.

Evidence of increased tolerance of the *like* usage in America comes from the contrast between the recommendation of Krapp (1927) that it should be avoided if only because it is so frequently condemned and the opposite advice given a few years ago by Pooley (1960), who, finding that present standards do not require the elimination of *like* as a conjunction, deliberately omitted the issue from his list of items on which teachers should give guidance. In between, the Leonard enquiry (1932) revealed a mixture of opinions; the majority rated the usage 'uncultivated'; but enough votes were cast in its favour for it to escape classification as 'illiterate' and to find a place in the 'disputable' zone.

British resistance has been stronger, though concessions have been made since Alford (1869) found the conjunctive *like* 'quite indefensible'. The Fowler brothers (1906) accorded it pride of place in their catalogue of 'vulgarisms and colloquialisms', and H. W. Fowler (1926) complained that 'every illiterate person uses this construction daily'. Partridge (1947) rates it not as an illiteracy but as at least a 'loose colloquialism'. But more recently attitudes have relaxed a little. If we follow Simeon Potter (1950) in being indulgent towards analogous creations, we might with him see 'Do *like* I do' as no worse than Elizabethan 'Do *like as* I do'. Gowers (1951) allows this *like* in colloquial English but not as regular British English prose; he firmly discriminates between 'Nothing succeeds *like* success' and 'Nothing succeeds *as* success *does*'. West and Kimber (1957) sit on the fence—' "Try to speak *like* I do" is becoming allowable, but is avoided by careful speakers and writers'—but Collins (1960) condemns the *like* conjunction outright, as does Golding (1964).

Our enquiry produced greater resistance than did Leonard's in America. By his measurement, the 24 per cent acceptance votes from our judges would have placed the item in his 'illiterate' category. It certainly came near the bottom (42nd of 50) of our order of acceptability. Tolerance by occupational groups followed the usual pattern, despite the comparatively narrow ranges involved (students 28 per cent, examiners 10 per cent acceptances).

ITEM 45. He told me the story and I *implied* a great deal from it.

This item is discussed in conjunction with Item 29 (pages 68–9 above).

ITEM 46. They bought some tomatoes *off* a barrow-boy.

The choice here—between *off* and *from*—is one of the least controversial of our list. The *O.E.D.* records that *off* is 'used idiomatically with many verbs, as Buy, Come, Dash, Get . . .', but few other authorities even mention it.

Though the American Lyman (1929) described the use of *off* for *from* as one of the seventeen most common errors in oral English, his countryman Leonard did not include this particular usage in his enquiry (1932). Leonard did, however, include *off of* (She leaped *off of* the moving car), and the response to this usage placed it in his 'disputable' category. One of the very few modern comments—and a decidedly cryptic one—is that of Collins (1960), who rules that *off* does not mean *from* and that consequently 'I took the ball *off* him' is wrong, by contrast with the correct 'I took the vase *off* the shelf'. It is by no means clear whether the critical distinction here is between the sense of removal from a position and that of transfer from person to person (i.e. a sort of inanimate/animate contrast), or whether it hinges on the presence or absence of the sense of 'taking *down*', or whether there is some other issue at stake.

Our respondents differentiated sharply between the four settings; the 'spread' ranged from 46 per cent acceptance in Informal Speech to a mere 3 per cent in Formal Writing (the overall average was 19 per cent). Only the merest handful of favourable votes were given in the two formal situations. This brought tolerance so low as to place the item 45th on the table of acceptability.

ITEM 47. It looked *like* it would rain.

The general observations under Item 44 (pages 94–5 above) on the propriety of using *like* as a conjunction apply to this usage, but the specific choice here is not between *like* and *as*, but between *like* and *as if*. For once the charge of Americanism may be to some extent justified; Krapp (1927) seems to testify to its comparative respectability when he comments that the construction 'It looks like rain' or 'It feels like rain' is a colloquial contraction of 'It looks like it would rain', etc.—though he probably means that it is a contracted collo-quialism. Marckwardt and Walcott (1938) say of the *O.E.D.* citations of this usage that the American ones are 'definitely colloquial'. In Leonard's enquiry (1932), one of the linguists remarked that 'The popular instinct in this and analogous uses of *like* is sound; it is more distinctive and clearer than *as*'; but even so only a quarter of the panel of judges accepted the expression, and Leonard concluded that it was, if not 'uncultivated', 'probably incorrect'. Follett (1966) uses the *as if* sense of *like* as an important aspect of his case for 'the futility of the argument from history'. Though *as if* was the primary meaning of *like* in 1400, this use is, in his view, 'even more repellent' than the simple use of *like* for *as*.

In England, Partridge (1947) illustrated his objection to *like* for *as if* from a novelist's 'Carted her out limp—looked *like* a chloroform-pad had been at work'. Gowers (1954) similarly condemns on behalf of English prose the alleged Americanism 'It looks *like* he was going to succeed'. Using statements about the weather, West and Kimber (1957), Collins (1960), and Lieberman (1964) all deplore sentences of the pattern 'It looks *like* it's going to rain/It looks *like* it were going to be fine/It looks *like* it might rain'.

Our judges were very unsympathetic. A general acceptance of only 12 per cent placed the item near the bottom of the poll (48th of 50). Though the students mustered nearly 50 per cent support in Informal Speech, even they very largely rejected the usage elsewhere. Not a single teacher, examiner or non-educationist voted favourably in either of the formal situations.

ITEM 48. I *will* be twenty-one tomorrow.

The distinction between *will* and *shall* (and between *would* and *should*) was described by Krapp (1927) as 'the great bugaboo of the English language'. Time has not helped much; very recently Follett (1966) found this issue to be 'as confused a jungle' as the user of English is ever called on to clear a way through. Some indication of its complexity is given by the number of pages devoted to it. The Fowlers (1906) used twenty-one, Jespersen (1909–1949) devoted well over one hundred and twenty to his survey, and Follett takes the whole matter out of his alphabetical 'lexicon' into a special twenty-three-page appendix.

Hall (1964) blames John Wallis (1653) for inventing 'the notorious *shall* and *will* rule, which has plagued English grammar ever since'. Fries (1940), commenting on the centuries of disagreement preceding current contradictory views, pushes the origin further back—to George Mason (1622) who, writing in French about English grammar, differentiated 'If I doe eate that, I *shall* be sicke' from 'If I doe eate that, I *will* be sicke'; the latter, he suggested, would have the unlikely sense of deliberate self-sickening ('. . . il sembleroit que volontairement vous volussiez estre malade'). According to Lounsbury (1908), the 'present distinction' was established by the middle of the seventeenth century—but only in England; it never gained the same currency in Scotland and Ireland, and it lost its hold in the United States. This geographical variation is confirmed by the *O.E.D.*, which records *will* for *shall* 'since 17th C, almost exclusively in Scottish, Irish, provincial, or extra-British use'.

Whenever and wherever the 'rules' were established, it was in eighteenth-century England that the most elaborate formulations flourished. Lindley Murray (1795) gave the full weight of his influential support to a set of rules adopted from William Ward (1765). The subtle complexity of the latter's exposition has a horrible fascination that makes it worth quoting at some length, if not in its full glory:

1. If the person who is represented as declaring a future state, or as having his thoughts declared, is both himself in the state, and likewise determines it; or if he is neither himself in the state, nor determines it, 'will' is used . . .

2. If the person who is represented as making a declaration, or as having his thoughts declared, concerning a future state, is either himself in it, but does not determine it, or is not himself in it, but does determine it, 'shall' is used.

As, 'I shall go—you say that you shall stay—John fears that he shall be undone . . . You shall go—you say that he shall stay—John determines that James shall be undone.'

It is little wonder that such a monstrous prescription failed to gain general acceptance, or that it provoked controversy. Fenning (1771) produced a simplification that has persisted down to modern times. According to him, in affirmative sentences first-person *shall* but second- and third-person *will* simply foretell, whereas the other forms promise or threaten; when the sentence is interrogative, the meanings are 'in general' directly the reverse. According to Leonard (1929), a yet simpler (though by no means easy) formula—that of Fell (1784)—came 'closer than anybody in either the eighteenth or nineteenth centuries to describing the time status of *shall* and *will*'. Fell considered the auxiliary *will* a mere sign of futurity, whereas *shall* conveyed a sense of something more—'obligation, possibility, contingency, or something conditional, and very often several of these together'. Only this kind of simplification can lend the slightest plausibility to Webster's claim that he never heard a wrong use of *shall* or *will* among American speakers of English.

The nationalistic note became a regular concomitant of the discussion. As Leonard remarks, 'no discussion of the *shall* and *will* matter in the latter part of the eighteenth century, as later, could get under way without condemnation of the Scotch and Irish for their misuses'. The familiar drowning anecdote today commonly told of a second-English speaker seems then to have featured a non-English Briton; it was a Scot or an Irishman who bawled out 'I *will* drown! Nobody *shall* save me!', thereby to the purist expressing a determination to die. But the Scots at least had a defender in James Beattie, Professor of Moral Philosophy at Aberdeen. In a whole text on this issue—*The Grammarian; or, The English Writer and Speaker's Assistant; comprising Shall and Will made easy to foreigners, with instances of their misuse on the part of natives of England* (1838)—he spurned both the above anecdote and Lindley Murray's 'vulgar notion' of differentiation by person (first/second as against third). Instead he advocated a rule as simple as Fell's in form, though making a rather different demarcation; he argued that *will* implies volition or not being influenced by the 'will' of another, while *shall* implies obligation, duty, necessity, or being influenced by the 'will' of another.

Alford (1869) entered the lists with a retort direct to the non-English and oblique to Webster's impeccable Americans; he claimed that he never knew an Englishman who misplaced *shall* and *will*, but had hardly ever known an Irishman or 'Scotchman' who did not do so sometimes. In insisting on first-person *shall* for mere futurity, he gives an example very like the purist's amendment of ours—'Next Tuesday I *shall* be twenty-one'. The scorn of the superior English for the 'Kelticism' of their nearest neighbours was expressed without inhibition at this time. Earle (2nd edition 1873) described the *shall, should/will, would* distinction as 'unerringly observed by the most rustic people in the purely English counties, while the most carefully educated persons who have grown up on Keltic soil cannot seize it!' Equally offensive was Grant White (1899), who referred to 'persons who have not had the advantage of early intercourse with educated people', such as 'Scotchmen', Irishmen and 'the great mass of the people of the Western and Southwestern States'. He none the less goes out of his way to refute a scholar named Marsh who had ventured the opinion that the *shall/will* distinction 'has, at present, no logical value or significance whatever', and had predicted 'that at no very distant day this verbal quibble will disappear, and that one of the auxiliaries will be employed with all persons of the nominative, exclusively as the sign of the future, and the other only as an expression of purpose or authority'. Stung by this, White acidly comments that 'any distinction is a quibble to persons too ignorant, too dull, or too careless for its apprehension'.

Twentieth-century developments in America tend to show Marsh as the more realistic of the two. Of Leonard's three *shall/will* items in his enquiry (1932), the one closest to ours—'I will probably come a little late'—secured approval from about two-thirds of his judges. From their comments Leonard concluded that 'probably what distinction ever has existed is gradually disappearing'. Fries (1940) draws a picture of uncertainty: 'Thus, after more than a century of discussion of the use of *shall* and *will*, there are no accepted views of what the actual usage of these two words is, of the meaning and trend of the development of that usage, and of the causes that gave rise to it.' But it could be argued that there is some evidence of a clear trend in American usage. Whereas Leonard's judges could not muster an acceptability of more than 75 per cent for any of his *shall/will* items, some years later Lewis (1949) got an 'Acceptability Ratio' of 90 per cent; in his survey 'the strict and ancient distinction' was approved by only 46 of 468 respondents. It was in this same year that Mencken— in the fourth edition of *The American Language*—gave the view that, 'except in the most painstaking and artificial varieties of American', the entire distinction 'may almost be said to have ceased to exist'. This line was reinforced by De Boer *et al.* (1951); their book for teachers of English included *shall/will* in a list of paired items which present and past usage had proved beyond all doubt to be 'completely interchangeable in cultivated English'. Similarly, Pooley (1960) observed that present standards do not require that there should be any distinction between *shall* and *will*, and excluded the usage from his list of items in which teachers should offer a model. It seems unlikely that the most recent attempt—by Follett (1966)—to rescue the old discrimination and prevent 'total surrender' will have much effect. His exploration of the territory where 'comparative law and order' prevail—an area where the difficulties are grouped under four heads (expressing plain future or set purpose; evidence of duplication; echoic auxiliaries in indirect discourse; anticipation of auxiliaries in questions)—is daunting enough. After a further ten pages about 'the realm of doubt and choice', where 'rule-defying idiom takes over', one admires his refusal to represent the difficulties as trifling or to claim that all the problems are soluble. At the same time, one doubts whether, even if 'with a little effort anyone can gain a command of the main principles and learn to bypass dilemmas', that effort is worth the making at this stage.

In twentieth-century England the old orthodoxy seems to have retained more of its hold than in America. The Fowlers (1906) thought that there was no real problem for 'southern Englishmen', to whom mastery of the *shall/will* usage 'comes by nature'. For the disadvantaged northerners they found that the short and simple directions often offered were worse than useless. Instead, they elaborated seven rules the mere titles of which—The Pure System, The Coloured-Future System, The Plain-Future System, Second-person Questions, Echoes, Substantival Clauses, Conditional Protasis and Indefinite Clauses—indicate what heavy weather could be made of the whole business. As if rather conscious of this, H. W. Fowler (1926) considerably condensed both the *shall/will* and the *should/would* issues, though still presenting six sections. In less formidable quarters, attempts have been made to preserve the old distinction. Barclay, Knox and Ballantyne (1945) reprint the traditional rulings about differentiation by person and by kind of utterance (statement, question, command). Vallins (1951) thinks that the whole business goes 'a little beyond the law', but clings to the view that, whereas in all persons but the first *will* is used for both simple future and 'determinative' tenses, the *shall/will* choice still operates in the first person. Gowers (1954) comes down in favour of the 'text-book orthodoxy' that still prescribes *shall* with the first person for the plain future. West and Kimber (1957) similarly require 'I *shall* grow old', because ageing is a phenomenon over which we have no control. Collins (1960) thinks that if—as seems possible—the 'rule' is decaying and *shall* and *will* are becoming interchangeable, 'certain subtleties of meaning are likely to disappear'. Golding (1964) repeats the traditional future tense paradigm with first-person *shall*. Barber (1964) points out—without the hint of disapproval that attends earlier noticing of the practice—that the abbreviated '*ll* form (e.g. *I'll* see you) often obviates difficult choice; in his view, where the full words are employed, the commoner *will* is spreading at the expense of *shall* and 'is likely to be the winner in any levelling process'.

The provocative character of this usage was also reflected in our judges' reactions. Comments were more frequent than usual, but, though most of them were adverse (e.g. 'I have never met just such a sentence—I mean one where the illogicality of this use of the modal verb is so clearly apparent'), the actual judgements were on the whole unexpectedly tolerant. This proved, in fact, to be one of the four items obtaining several majority votes; on the average over the four situations, most of the students, teachers and non-educationists (as well as nearly half the lecturers) registered tolerance. The overall acceptance rate was 56 per cent, placing the usage 11th in the acceptability table. Examiners (37 per cent approval) were conspicuously harsher than the others. In all groups other than theirs the 'spread' of reaction between Informal Speech and Formal Writing was very wide.

ITEM 49.   **Everyone has *their* off-days.**

English lacks a common-sex singular pronoun. Speakers or writers embarked upon a sentence like the above are confronted with a choice between the strictly grammatical but cumbersome *his or her* and a more convenient plural form (e.g. *they, their*) which defies concord. As might be expected, the latter has been commonly condemned and even more commonly used. The *O.E.D.*'s citations date from 1420 ('Iche mon in *thayre* degree') to 1898 (Shaw's 'It's enough to drive anyone out of *their* senses'). Jane Austen, Leonard reminds us, 'uniformly employs this usage', and Curme (1931) quotes examples similar to ours—though adding the opinion that the singular pronouns or adjectives would be preferred nowadays—from Fielding, Defoe, Addison, and Beaconsfield.

In America Leonard's survey (1932) included the item 'Everybody bought *their* own tickets'. Although many judges approved of it, the majority against it was large enough to rate it 'disputable'. Lewis (1949) obtained similar results; a 45 per cent acceptance of 'Everyone put on *their* coats', with only professors giving it a majority vote, ranked it as controversial. A few years later Gorrell and Laird (1953) found 'everyone . . . *their*' common colloquially and sometimes acceptable in writing, though avoided by careful writers. Such avoidance can, however, produce odd results, as Leonard (1929) illustrates with a child's over-correct account of being ducked while swimming: 'When I came up, everybody was laughing at me, but I was glad to see *him* just the same.'

In England resistance has been firmer. The Fowlers (1906) express the view, admittedly disputable, that *they, their*, etc., should never be resorted to in this kind of construction. They correct *their* to *his* in (for example) Beaconsfield's 'Everybody is discontented with *their* lot in life'. H. W. Fowler (1926), insisting on the singular pronoun, rather unconvincingly argues that the 'wrong' usage (e.g. Thackeray's 'A person can't help *their* birth') has an 'old-fashioned sound' that suggests that the cause of the grammarians will triumph. For Partridge (1947) the plural, though common, is an error. Vallins (1951), though in general condemning inconsistency of number, is not unwilling to pass '*nearly everyone* has opinions about modern questions even if *their* knowledge of them . . .', on the ground that, paradoxically, *nearly everyone* has 'a plurality that does not belong to the simple everyone'. Gowers (1954) is sympathetic to the problem, but recommends official writers not to be tempted by the greater convenience of the plural *their*. Collins (1960) and Berry (1963) categorically condemn the mixed number usage as wrong, but West and Kimber (1957) allow it 'in an informal context' (e.g. 'Everybody took *their* partners') and Golding (1964), with unusual leniency, even allows that such sentences (e.g. 'Everyone should play *their* part') are now accepted as correct.

Not surprisingly, our respondents differentiated sharply between Informal Speech and Formal Writing, with acceptance rates of 72 per cent and 19 per cent respectively. The average 42 per cent put the item in the upper half of the acceptability table (20th of 50). The pattern of response by occupational groups was near the standard; the most tolerant group—students—was nearly twice as well-disposed as the least so—examiners.

ITEM 50.   **They will *loan* you the glasses.**

Is *loan* acceptable as a verb? There is no doubt that in this country it once was—at least as early as the sixteenth century. The very earliest *O.E.D.* citations (e.g. 'Gif ðu him *lanst* ani þing of ðinen', *c.* 1200) may belong to *to lend* rather than *to loan*, but later ones conclusively demonstrate the respectable ancestry of the latter. According to Fowler (1926) 'The verb has been expelled from idiomatic southern English by *lend*, but was formerly correct, and survives in U.S. and locally in U.K.'

The American survival seems to have been in a subsidiary role; Krapp (1927) describes it as 'not as general as *lend*, and avoided by some speakers and writers as a crudity'. Leonard's investigation (1932) elicited a strong majority in its favour, with 195 of the 229 judges approving it; 'a quarter considered it acceptable as formal or literary English'. Hence the verdict of Partridge (1947)—'good American'—

to which he adds 'but not yet good English'. In discussing a different verb—*to contact*—Gowers (1954) prophesies that it will establish itself on the strength of the precedent set by verbs like *loan*, which 'is trying to come back again, after a long holiday, spent ... in America'. The prejudice against it, however, is by no means dead; Lieberman (1964) condemns it and substitutes *lend*.

Our judges' reactions suggest that it may be long before *to loan* is generally accepted. A mere 22 per cent of votes were cast in its favour, so rating its acceptability very low (43rd out of 50). Even students managed to average only 27 per cent acceptance. Compared with other occupational groups, non-educationists were distinctly less tolerant, and teachers more so, than usual.

ITEM 51.   **He jumped *onto* the roof of the shed.**

Feeling that the difference in speech between *on to* and *onto* is by no means always detectable by the ear, we confined our enquiry to written usage. In this connexion the *O.E.D.* (1933) remarks that, though the need for the single word *onto* was felt before the sixteenth century, its recognition in writing is still quite recent and limited. Citations start from 1819, with Keats's 'Please you walk forth Onto the Terrace'.

Despite the analogy with the *into/in to* pair and the convenience—emphasized, for example, by West and Kimber (1957)—of using *onto* (like *into*) for motion by contrast with *on* (and *in*) for position, there has been marked reluctance to recognize *onto*. Krapp (1927) reports that in America 'printers, publishers and rhetoricians for the most part do not countenance *onto* and insist on printing or writing as two words'. In England Fowler (1926) concedes rather grudgingly that there are occasions when *onto* is justifiable, but usually as an alternative to the single *on* or *to*. With a sentence very similar to ours, he accepts *on* or *to* or *onto*—'but on no account *on to*'—in 'climbed up *on(to)* the roof'. While sensibly urging writers and printers to make up their minds about *onto*—'Abstain from the preposition if you like; use it and own up if you like; but do not use it and pretend there is no such word'—he seems implicitly to favour the first of these alternatives, abstention. A more recent tendency to accept *onto*, when appropriate, is reflected in Partridge (1947) and in Collins (1960); the latter allows as correct 'He climbed *onto* the roof'.

As with *into/in to*, a distinction may be observed between the purely prepositional *onto* and the preposition *to* preceded by a phrasal verb using the particle *on*, e.g. between 'walked/*onto* the platform', and 'walked *on/to* the next station'. Such a distinction does not arise with our sentence. The 53 per cent acceptance of our written *onto* usage compares favourably with most of the main fifty items. Presumably, if it had been feasible to present it also in speech, the acceptability rate would have taken it near the top of the list. Even so, the percentage of rejections is quite considerable.

ITEM 52. *Who* **was he looking for?**
Rightly or wrongly we thought this so obviously a speech usage (we would hesitate to commit ourselves now!) that it would hardly be encountered in formal, though it might occur in informal, writing: we therefore posed only the first three 'situations'. The italicizing was intended to indicate that the issue was not that of the 'final preposition' but the choice between interrogative *who* and *whom* in initial position. Our view of the dilemma has since been well expressed by Follett (1966): 'The objective form of the pronoun *who* is having a hard time asserting its hereditary rights. On one side it suffers the mistreatment of those who will put the *-m* in where it does not belong, out of fear of being thought uneducated; on the other, it is belabored by emancipated grammarians who find it bookish and affected in most uses and favour almost any construction that avoids it.'

The *O.E.D.* cites instances of 'ungrammatical' *who* for *whom* from the Paston Letters onwards—including Cranmer's '*Who* should your grace trust hereafter?', Shakespeare's '*Who* joyn'st thou with?', and Hardy's '*Who* are you speaking of?' Leonard (1929) assembles eighteenth-century views, with Lowth positive for the strict 'rule', but others—e.g. Priestley—finding *who* so commonly defying the rule, especially in conversation, that it should be accepted. Not all agree on which is the rule, which the exception. Webster (1789), for example, argues that '*whom* do you speak *to*?' is not only never said but is 'hardly English at all'. In his view *who* is equivalent to the Latin dative *cui* and was unquestioned 'until some Latin student began to suspect it bad English, because not agreeable to the Latin rules. At any rate, *whom* do you speak *to*? is a corruption, and all the grammars that can be found will not extend the use of the phrase beyond the walls of a college.' The Grammar (1771) of a British contemporary, Fenning, also defended the *who* form, and without reference to Latin, on the simple ground that 'A Preposition does not always govern the oblique case; as, *Who* is this for? *Who* did you give it to?' For this audacity he was taken to task by the Newcastle grammarian Joshua Story

(3rd edition 1783), who accused him of producing 'two barbarisms to prove the truth of a false rule', and insisted that the ungrammatical, even vulgar, character of Fenning's proposition was revealed by the objectionable transpositions 'For who . . .', 'To who . . .', Knowles (4th edition 1796) supports this objection by including '*Who* should I meet?' in his list of Improper Expressions.

The dispute is still very much alive in the twentieth century. The Fowlers (1906), while conceding that 'Who . . .?' is less bookish and more genial, advise 'the correct forms' for print other than dialogue. H. W. Fowler (1926) finds no further defence than 'colloquial' is needed for *who* in talk. In America, Sapir (1921) gives ten pages of his chapter on 'Drift' to the *who/whom* question. To him the interesting feature is 'the larger tendencies at work in the language', which this usage problem illustrates. The levelling of the distinction between subjective and objective forms is 'but a late chapter in the steady reduction of the old Indo-European system of syntactic cases'. He identifies four powerful influences favouring *who* in initial position: first, the pull towards an invariable form corresponding to *which, what, that*; second, psychological affinity with invariable interrogative adverbs (e.g. *where, when, how*); third, the 'territorial' association of pre-verbal position with subjective case-form; and fourth, the avoidance of the rhetorical 'drag' of the final *-m* of *whom*, slowing down the movement of the sentence. Support of this view comes from Leonard's study (1932), which categorized '*Who* are you looking for?' as established usage, and from Fries (1940), whose Standard English materials yielded no examples of *whom* but a number of *who* as the usual interrogative form. The judges consulted by Lewis (1949) were less lenient. Though most of his professors, lexicographers and authors were tolerant, his teachers heavily opposed it; with a mere 43 per cent of favourable votes, it classed itself as controversial. Lewis quotes a colleague's provocative comment that 'You can always tell a half-educated buffoon by the care he takes in working the word [i.e. *whom*] in'.

British views, which are also mixed, tend to greater caution. Low and Hollingworth (1941) condemn '*Who* . . . to look for?' in written English. Partridge (1947) condemns similar written usages, but admits that *whom* sounds pedantic in speech. Vallins (1951) quotes a letter to the *Times Educational Supplement* by P. B. Ballard; it describes as 'a piece of linguistic swank' the 'over-correct' use of *whom* by people who, 'knowing little or nothing about grammar, regard *whom* as a more scholarly and more dignified word than *who*'. In his supplementary volume (1953), Vallins quotes another correspondent who complains about the enormous increase in the past twenty-five years in 'the distressing misuse of *who* and *whom*'. Gowers (1954) pleads for the 'correct' distinction; he, too, quotes a press letter, from 'A. Woodcock': 'Regarding the suggested disuse of *whom*, may I ask by who a lead can be given? To who, to wit, of the "cultured" authorities can we appeal to boo *whom* and to boom *who*?' (The hooting echo of '*to who(m)*' was also exploited by Ambrose Bierce, in a jingle—quoted by Follett—about the decline of love-making among men and owls:

> Sitting singly in the gloaming and no longer two and two;
> As unwilling to be wedded as unpracticed how to woo;
> With regard to being mated
> Asking still with aggravated
> Ungrammatical acerbity: "To who? To who?").

Most recently, on both sides of the Atlantic, the balance seems to have shifted in favour of *who*. Both West and Kimber (1957) and Pooley (1960) find '*Who* did he give it to?' acceptable in all but very formal situations; in the latter '*To whom . . . ?*' is preferable to '*Whom . . . to?*'. Lieberman (1964), however, favours the second ('hybrid') construction by amending *who* in '*Whom* are you laughing at?'.

Our judges were tolerant of this usage, allowing it 68 per cent acceptability in the three situations posed. Though the inclusion of Formal Writing would presumably have reduced the acceptance rate, it might not have done so very severely; several respondents claimed that they would have employed the *who*-usage even in Formal Writing. There was not much to choose between the older groups, all of which averaged out at 60–70 per cent acceptance, but the students (73 per cent) were distinctly more lenient. Incidentally, examiners were, by a slight margin, the second most lenient group.

ITEM 53. **That's a dangerous curve; you'd better go *slow*.**
The defenders of adverbial *slow* see it as one of a number of 'flat' adverbs; another is *quick*, the comparative form of which (*quicker*) was discussed under Item 32. The *O.E.D.* supports adverbial *slow* with quotations from, for example, Shakespeare (How *slow* this old moon wanes), Milton (swinging *slow*), and Thackeray (We drove very *slow*). Pooley (1946) points out that, in early English, adverbs were formed from adjectives in two ways—by adding *-lic* or *-e*; the 'flat' form derived from the latter is just as 'correct' and as 'native' as the

8

-ly form from the former. To disallow such an 'ancient and dignified part of our language' as the adverbial *slow* is—as Greenough and Kittredge (1902) say—a pedantry not to be encouraged. Fowler (1926) protests against the encroachments of *-ly*; he defends 'Please read very *slow*', and finds *slower* and *slowest* preferable to *more/most slowly*. He further makes a subtle distinction between 'We forged *slowly* ahead' (where the slowness is 'an unessential item') and 'Sing as *slow* as you can' (where the slowness is 'all that matters'). It would perhaps need more than Fowler's ingenuity to apply this distinction to the line quoted by Pooley (1946) from a poem by Clough—'In front the sun climbs slow, how slowly'.

The American Krapp (1927) dismissed as 'entirely artificial' the 'rule' that all adverbs must end in *-ly*; its falsity is illustrated by *soon*. Leonard (1932) used our own sentence in addition to two other *slow* constructions. Of his judges 15 per cent approved the usage as formal literary English, 15 per cent condemned it as illiterate, and the rest approved it as colloquial; on balance, this voting placed it in the 'established' category. Lewis's survey (1949) confirmed this classification; with only 75 of 468 respondents rejecting it, it scored 84 per cent approval.

In England, Partridge (1947)—as already noted under Item 32— rates the *-ly* form more polite, the root form more vigorous. But Hornby (1954) welcomes the latter only in the semi-strike situation of 'go slow'; elsewhere, he thinks the *-ly* form the usual one, as in 'Drive *slowly* round the bend'. West and Kimber (1957) make the same distinction, but Gowers (1954) classes 'drive slow' with a number of shibboleths once supposed to distinguish the well- from the ill-educated. (In this case, the former avoided the usage.)

Hindsight makes our restriction of this item to the two informal situations seem rather odd; perhaps we over-hastily identified the informal with the conversational. Even so, the usage was accepted in only 54 per cent of judgements; the inclusion of formal contexts would presumably have seriously reduced this figure. Acceptance in Informal Writing was distinctly less than two-thirds of acceptance in Informal Speech. The order of group-tolerance was unusual, with examiners (67 per cent) most lenient, teachers (46 per cent) least so, and students (52 per cent) less tolerant than the average for the whole group.

ITEM 54. **In spite of the delay, everything was *alright*.**

Is *alright* a valid word at all, or is it a mistake for *all right*? Many of those who denounce the single word treat it as a corrupt novelty, though it might equally well be considered as a revival. The *O.E.D.* records Old English '*Alrihtes* swa alse þe wise teolie . . . nimeð ȝeme of twam þingen' (about 1175) and, from the *Ancrene Riwle* (*c.* 1230), '*alriht* so'. That this form may have completely disappeared at one time is suggested by the absence of reference to it by many scholars. The American Krapp (1927) implies awareness of the historical 'drift' in his comment that *all right* is now never written as one word, *alright*, and was rarely so written at any time. But Fowler (1926) suggests that the single word is a modern phenomenon; he insists that there are no such forms as *all-right*, *allright*, or *alright* and attributes the frequency of the last to analogical confusion with *already* and *altogether*.

Leonard (1932) did not submit *alright* to his judges, but he did invite reactions to 'That will be *all right*, you may be sure'. This reminds us that the two-word form is not above reproach. His judges were tolerant enough to rate it as 'established', and only 5 of over 200 condemned it as 'vulgar'. But clearly one must allow the possibility that a few objections to *alright* might be directed against the colloquial character of both it and its two-word alternative.

In more recent times, English writers have tended to reject *alright*. Partridge (1947) thinks it a mis-spelt and illogical variant of *all right*. (It is not easy to see how logic comes into the issue.) Vallins (1951) describes the one-word form as an 'unlawful union', and Collins (1960) gives the somewhat unrealistic ruling that 'there is no such word'. One would expect modern linguists to accept *alright*, but at least one— the American Sledd (1962)—singles it out for attack. He has, he says, 'few complaints about spelling, the only loud one being against *alright*'.

At least one of our respondents, without giving evidence or argument, thought the single form 'predominantly American'. A few saw it as a reasonable analogical formation, though still possibly irritating. Assuming that the distinction between one-word and two-word forms would not necessarily be detectable in speech, we asked only about written usage. In Informal Writing, it was voted acceptable by more than half (55 per cent), but this figure dropped to well under a third in Formal Writing. Examiners were noticeably harsher than any other group, though teachers mustered only 15 per cent tolerance in the formal situation.

ITEM 55.   **Between you and *I*, she drinks heavily.**

The issue here is clear-cut: is the subjective form *I* permissible after the preposition *between*? As far as possible, discussion will be restricted to this specific issue, though it is obviously related to the choice of pronominal form after a verb (e.g. Item 42: 'She told Charles and *I* . . .'). To those brought up on traditional grammar there is little doubt that 'between you and *me*' is the only acceptable construction, and in an unguarded moment we allowed conventional bias against the test-form *I* to persuade us to exclude the Formal Writing situation. For this rashness, some of our respondents—including one very well-known expert—justly rebuked us.

The *O.E.D.* reminds us that, though 'between you and *I*' is now considered ungrammatical, it was not always so; in fact, it was very frequent in the seventeenth and latter part of the sixteenth centuries. The dictionary quotes, as do others, Antonio's 'All debts are cleared between you and *I*' (*Merchant of Venice*), and suggests that the aberration, if such it is, may be encouraged by the separation of the questionable form from the preposition. Partridge (1947) blames the invariability of *you*, which fails to signal distinctive case, so that people who would never say 'between *he* and *I*' do say 'between *you* and *I*'. Another factor may be placing of *you and I* in positions where a following verb may generate the feeling that subjective case is appropriate. The commonest such situation perhaps occurs after *let*; in 'Let you and *I* do it' the pronominal pair may be intuitively felt as subject of *do* rather than object of *let*. Yet another element might be the all-too-familiar phenomenon of over-correction. Gowers (1954), for instance, argues that ferocity in correcting the opposite error (*me* for *I* in, e.g., Lydia Bennet's 'Mrs. Forster and *me* are such good friends') has induced a conviction that 'such combinations as *you and me* are in all circumstances ungrammatical'. The American Dwight Macdonald (1962), by no means a 'permissivist', has sadly reported that 'the chief result of the long crusade against "It's me" is that most Americans now say "Between you and I . . ." '.

This crusade doubtless flourished, along with all the others, in the eighteenth century. But the test-usage was not without its defenders. They included Archibald Campbell, from whose *Lexiphanes* (second edition 1767) Leonard makes the interesting quotation: 'In the first Edition of this work, I had used the phrase *between you and I*, which tho' it must be confessed to be ungrammatical, is yet almost universally used in familiar conversation, and sometimes by our best comick writers: see Wycherley's *Plain Dealer*. This very trivial slip, if it be one, has not escaped the diligence and sagacity of the learned and candid Reviewers. One of our worthy labourers in that periodical drudgery has declared this phrase, and a few others, which are only improper in his crazy imagination, to be more offensive to a judicious reader, than all the hard words I had attempted to expose.'

The victory of the 'grammatical' point of view was resounding enough for condemnations of the *I* usage to predominate still in twentieth-century usage handbooks. The Fowlers (1906) thought it 'a bad blunder', though a common one in talk. Henry Fowler (1926) even denied it that status of 'colloquial usage' which lent some respectability to 'the contrary lapse' of 'It is *me*'. At much the same time in America, however, Krapp (1927) allowed 'between you and *I*' (though not the best English) to occur 'occasionally in colloquial speech'. A generation later, and in England, Vallins (1951) conceded that the particular phrase under consideration 'has become almost standardized in modern usage', though the construction it used was none the less an error. Elsewhere, straight condemnation is the commonest reaction. For Collins (1960), 'between you and *I*' is wrong, is not permissible in either speech or writing, and is to be avoided at all costs. Berry (1963), Lieberman (1964) and Golding (1964) all flatly reject the *I* usage. On the other hand, and conceivably with more realism, modern linguists are more tolerant. Halliday *et al.* (1964), for instance, express the view that 'telling the child that he must say *between you and me* and not *between you and I*, or vice versa, because the one is "better" or "clearer" than the other corresponds to nothing in his experience of language'.

Even without the Formal Writing category, our judges rated this usage very low. An acceptance of 23 per cent places it near the bottom of the acceptability table; with a Formal Writing assessment it would surely have come last or nearly last. In no area did it attract a majority in favour, though the non-educationists—for once more lenient than the students—gave it 48 per cent votes in Informal Speech. Examiners were extremely harsh; only two of the thirty-five tolerated the usage in any circumstances.

5

Some implications for the teaching of English

We have been exploring what someone has called 'the briar patch of English usage'. Certainly the terrain is full of tangled thickets. In itself it is only a tiny 'patch' of language, but not quite as (so?) small as is sometimes argued. According to Davies—in Wilkinson (1965)— the 'region of uncertainty' contains a mere 40-odd items. In our view the figure is distinctly higher; most of our 55 items are still controversial, many of them represent whole families of similar usages, and our respondents readily added a hundred or two more. We would also question Davies's contention that it can be made perfectly clear to children, not only that a small number of items are in dispute, but also that 'in each case, this and not that is the one normally used'. Our evidence of theory and practice in usage suggests that the problem is more variable and uncertain than that.

Of much greater interest and concern, however, is the possibility that some of the features conspicuous in the treatment of our few particular items may be characteristic of more general attitudes to language. Both in the historical survey and in some of the answers to the questionnaire we found what seemed to be indications of pedantry, of prejudice, of readiness to pontificate, and of unrealistic conservatism. Teachers and other educationists (including ourselves) are obviously no more exempt from these weaknesses than others. (Many of our own dubious assumptions have been salutarily exposed as quite unjustified.) If, as seems reasonable to expect, the teacher of English ought to give— directly or indirectly—a measure of guidance on verbal behaviour, how can he guard against inconsistency, arbitrariness, prejudice and ineffectiveness? How can he be less negatively inhibiting and more positively encouraging than so many of the grammarians of the past and manual-writers of the present?

One obvious requirement is that he should base his advice and guidance on knowledge of the facts, present and past. For the present situation, apart from the necessarily limited information offered by surveys such as ours, he can but keep his eyes and ears open. Only by so doing can he remain sensitive to linguistic change. Otherwise, he may go on fighting rearguard actions (e.g. against prepositional 'due to') long after the battle is over; he may likewise allow the gap between his recommendations and the actual usage of others (not to mention his own actual usage) to become too wide to be spanned. As for the past, he may well find awful warnings in history, in the shape of centuries of *ex cathedra* pronouncements uttered with a degree of conviction only matched by the completeness of their subsequent oblivion. If further deterrent examples are needed beyond those we have already mentioned, they can readily be found in the correspondence columns of literary journals. The temptation to dogmatize is considerably reduced, for instance, by study of the 'retained object' controversy of little more than fifty years ago; a writer to *Notes and Queries* in 1911 was prompted by this (to him) distressingly frequent solecism to reassert the rule that in the passive transformation the indirect object of the verb transitive can never become the subject, so that construction of the type 'I was told the story . . .' are 'at once ungrammatical and illogical'. An even odder-sounding 'rule' from a generation earlier was revived by a correspondent of the *London Quarterly Review* in 1874—'the possessive case must not be substituted for the preposition *of*, unless *possession* is implied by it'; thus 'its course' is proper when speaking of a river but objectionable in reference to a speech, and Shakespeare's 'deep damnation of his taking off' is to be explained only by 'poetical license'. Teachers of English are sometimes and with some justice accused of lack of curiosity about the language they teach; an exploration of the historical byways of usage controversy can be recommended as fascinating in itself and as a healthy corrective of premature certainty.

The teacher who was himself taught old-fashioned prescriptive grammar and who, because of the neglect of language study—at least until recently—in many institutions of higher education, has not studied the language systematically since 'O' Level may well find the weight of his commitments a severe disincentive to the revival of such study. His reluctance might be intensified by the suspicion that he would be forced to realize that language behaviour is infinitely more complex than the simple, monolithic model he was brought up on.

Nevertheless, if his teaching is to be effective, he cannot afford to neglect the truth, even if it seems to be making his job more subtle and difficult.

To add to the complexity, the teacher must take into account not only the facts neutrally recorded by the academic linguist but also social and psychological considerations where objective neutrality is not enough. To make clear the social facts of language levels and 'registers' is necessary but not sufficient; the teacher must also help his pupils to move among them in a socially acceptable way. For example, he may demolish in the most scientific fashion the myth that condemns the 'split infinitive', and yet go on—as indeed one American linguist (R. A. Hall, 1964) recommends—to advise against splitting, on social rather than linguistic grounds, pointing out that however reasonable it is to 'split', it may arouse emotions of hostility that more than offset its reasonableness.

An example of a psychological complication is the tendency for the young learner to demand greater certainty than the linguistic facts allow. In an analysis of the work of I. A. Richards, Hotopf (1965) records that Richards 'attributed the prevalence of the normative attitude to language largely to teachers, because of their influence over the young', but argues that this is unfair to teachers. Even if they taught differently, 'we should probably still have the ontogenetic recapitulation of the eighteenth-century's attitude to language in everybody's life history'. On the evidence of Piaget and others, children go through 'an absolutist stage in their attitude to rules and will do so no matter what their teachers say'. Perhaps the growing science of psycho-linguistics will help teachers both to meet this initial need of children and to ensure that they do in fact get through the absolutist stage.

At a more practical and immediate level two recommendations on attitudes to disputed usage occur to us. The first is that we might less often assume that where two or more alternatives confront us there is necessarily one 'preferred' usage that we ought consistently to select. With many of our items it hardly seems to matter which choice is made. If we can live comfortably—as we seem to do—with alternative spellings of words like *judg(e)ment* or *realise/realize* and with rival pronunciations of words like *controversy*, why should we not tolerate equally *averse to/averse from*, *under* or *in the circumstances*, *different from*, *to* or even *than*, *between you and me* or *I*, and so on? Even where the point at issue is possible ambiguity (e.g. disinterested/uninterested, implied/inferred), it is remarkably difficult to misunderstand any full piece of discourse in which the forms are used 'wrongly'.

Our final recommendation would be a resolution to try and (to?) 'lower the temperature'. Language usage is so personal a matter that we are all, children no less than adults, acutely sensitive to charges of incorrectness, illiteracy, oddness or—above all—social inferiority in our choice of words. Here again our historical survey offers a warning. It shows that 'Americanism' is not the only emotionally-loaded pejorative expression of tribalism. Few of us can be sure that we are proof against the accusation of Briticism, Celticism, Scotticism or Irishism. Even more chastening to us in the north is the regionalism which assumes the superiority of southern English—the view of the Fowler brothers, for example (see page 101), that mastery of the *shall/will* distinction comes by nature only to Southern Englishmen. The dangers in the classroom of making this kind of geographical discrimination, and still more of making the social-class discrimination often linked with it, are obvious.

*   *   *

Language behaviour is an inexhaustible topic. We must limit ourselves to these few samples of the reflections provoked by our enquiry. We feel amply rewarded for our labours by the fascination of the subject itself, and still more by the corrective influence it has exercised on us. Many of our brash assumptions have been undermined, and our respect for the toughness and resilience of the English language (despite the mauling it receives at the hands of the theorists of usage) has been much enhanced. If readers get from the material presented a fraction of the interest and educative value that we think we have experienced, the enquiry will have been worth while.

In conclusion, we are grateful to the Institute of Education of Newcastle University for sponsoring the project, to Miss Evelyn Chatt (the Institute's Research Secretary) for patiently typing successive drafts, and above all to those who completed the questionnaires in the first instance.

W. H. MITTINS
MARY SALU
MARY EDMINSON
SHEILA COYNE

Appendix: Additional items

We invited respondents to supplement our list with 'any items of similar interest'. To us, this meant items that might reasonably have been used in our questionnaire. Unfortunately, our terse wording largely failed to communicate this sense. We were also at fault in not asking for the suggestions to be accompanied by judgements of acceptability. As a result, though a few people inferred our meaning, far more used the opportunity to present usages they seemed to find in some degree reprehensible. This in itself, however, was an interesting indication of the strength of concern about matters of usage, as well as confirmation of the tendency towards prohibition that we detected in responses to the questionnaire.

Among the several hundred items offered, a small number presented the sort of balanced dilemma we had in mind. (Some of our own items in fact were much less balanced.) The most popular single example of this kind was the use of 'aggravating' for 'annoying'. Others were:

> compared to/with
> consist in/of
> centre round/on
> Your sex are/is illogical
> The man who(m) we thought was . . .
> final prepositions
> the popular use of 'nice'.

In our view—of course subjective and therefore biased—the alternatives are less evenly balanced in:

> a large amount (number?) of people
> quite a few (a number of?)
> several cherubims
> five foot (feet?) high
> littler, littlest.

To this list might perhaps be added a number of popular usages apparently offered for condemnation rather than debate. For example:

colloquialisms	—	know-how
		to face up to
		aren't I?
Americanisms	—	do you have?
		sidewalk
		okay
		desegregation (for 'integration')
regionalisms	—	a *soon* train
		to *seek* some coal
		there's a stupid thing to do
		I have *a* one

jargon and cliché — to contact
at your earliest convenience
this day and age
by and large
a good buy.

Similar usages where the alternative is less obvious include:
it's up to you
to finalize
teenager
strength-wise, money-wise (and the like).

The alternative would seem to be zero (i.e. omission of the objectionable form) in tautologies such as 'I myself...', 'Personally I...', 'Definitely yes'.

Still more difficult, perhaps impossible, to handle would be usages where the preferred alternative might be distinctly circuitous, e.g.:
the caravan *sleeps* four
the settee *sits* three
to *catch* a bus.

An objection to 'heavily pre-modified nouns' similarly discounts the difficulty of finding neat alternatives, though the particular example given (a high-speed low-engine-capacity sports car) hardly attracts defence.

A number of other items seem to us to present choices which are clear but unimportant. Should we not tolerate graphological alternatives such as 'the 1960s' or 'the 1960's' and the variant 'show/shew' spellings? If so, our leniency might be stretched to cover in many circumstances:
all of a sudden (for 'suddenly')
firstly (for 'first')
I *lit* a match
Go and *get ready*
The time is *just on* three o'clock.

Finally, and at the risk of betraying ignorance or obtuseness, we feel bound to record that some usages submitted as objectionable or at least debatable strike us as so normal that we cannot understand why they are mentioned. Among these items are:
Let him *be*
to avoid *any unnecessary* correspondence
Please return it *as soon as possible*
from whom I have *learned* much
a *modified* version (of a car)
the former and the latter (allegedly a 'shocking device').

Nevertheless, we are as grateful for these suggestions as for all the others.

References

(The reader will appreciate that the following list includes, not only scholarly works on language, but reference books of widely different value and also texts from which little more than brief comments or examples have been quoted. On balance, it seemed neater to present a single, if rather indiscriminate, list than to separate the various categories of work or to make extensive use of footnotes.)

ALFORD, H. (1869) *A Plea for the Queen's English* (London: Strahan).

ALLEN, H. B. (ed.) (1958) *Readings in Applied English Linguistics* (New York: Appleton-Century).

BAKER, R. (1770) *Reflections on the English Language;* (1779) 2nd edition titled 'Remarks on . . .' (London: Bell).

BALLARD, P. B. (1939) *Teaching and Testing English* (London: U.L.P.).

BARBER, C. (1964) *Linguistic Change in Present-Day English* (Edinburgh: Oliver & Boyd).

BARCLAY, J., KNOX, D. H. & BALLANTYNE, G. B. (1945) *A Study of Standard English* (Glasgow: Gibson).

BEATTIE, J. (1838) *The Grammarian; or, The English Writer and Speaker's Assistant; comprising Shall and Will made easy to foreigners, with instances of their misuse on the part of the natives of England* (London).

BERRY, T. E. (1963) (first English edition) *The Most Common Mistakes in English Usage* (London: Pitman).

CAMPBELL, G. (1776) *The Philosophy of Rhetoric* (London: Strahan).

COLLEGE ENTRANCE EXAMINATION BOARD: COMMISSION ON ENGLISH (1965) *Freedom and Discipline in English* (New York: C.E.E.B.).

COLLINS, — (1960) *Collins' Everyday English Usage* (ed. Thomson and Irvine) (London: Collins).

CURME, G. O. (1931) *Syntax* (Vol. 3 of *A Grammar of the English Language*) (Boston: Heath).

DAVIES, H. SYKES (1951) *Grammar Without Tears* (London: Bodley Head).

DEAN, L. F., & WILSON, K. G. (ed.) (1959) 2nd edition 1963 *Essays on Language and Usage* (New York: O.U.P.).

DE BOER, J. J., KAULFERS, W. V. & MILLER, H. R. (1951) *Teaching Secondary English* (New York: McGraw-Hill).

EARLE, J. (1871) 2nd edition 1873 *The Philosophy of the English Tongue* (Oxford: Clarendon).

FELL, J. (1784) *Essay Towards an English Grammar* (London: Dilly).

FENNING, D. (1771) *A New Grammar of the English Language* (London: Crowder).

FOLLETT, WILSON (1960) *Grammar is Obsolete* (Atlantic Monthly, 1960); (1966) *Modern American Usage* (U.S.A.: Longmans). (Edited and completed, after Follett's death, by Jacques Barzun in collaboration with others.)

FOWLER, H. W., & FOWLER, F. G. (1906) *The King's English* (London: O.U.P.).

FOWLER, H. W. (1926) *A Dictionary of Modern English Usage* (London: O.U.P.).

FRIES, C. C. (1940) *American English Grammar* (New York: Appleton-Century).

GOLDING, S. R. (1964) *Common Errors in English Language* (London: Macmillan).

GORRELL, R. M., & LAIRD, C. (1953) *Modern English Handbook* (New York: Prentice-Hall).

GOWERS, SIR E. (1948) *Plain Words: A Guide to the Use of English* (H.M.S.O.); (1951) *A B C of Plain Words* (H.M.S.O.); (1954) *The Complete Plain Words* (H.M.S.O.) ('—in the main a reconstruction of my two previous books').

GREENOUGH, J. B., & KITTREDGE, G. L. (1902) *Words and their Ways in English Speech* (New York: Macmillan).

GREENWOOD, J. (1711) *An Essay towards a Practical English Grammar* (London: Tookey).

HALL, FITZEDWARD (1873) *Modern English* (London: Williams and Norgate); (1917) *English Usage* (London: Williams and Norgate).

HALL, J. LESSLIE (1917) *English Usage: Studies in the history and uses of English words and phrases* (Chicago: Scott, Foresman and Co.).

HALL, R. A. (1960) *Linguistics and Your Language* (New York: Anchor). (This is a second, revised edition of the author's *Leave Your Language Alone!*, 1950); (1964) *Introductory Linguistics* (Philadelphia: Chilton).

HALLIDAY, M. A. K., McINTOSH, A. & STREVENS, P. D. (1964) *The Linguistic Sciences and Language Teaching* (London: Longmans).

HARRIS, G. (1752) *Observations upon the English Language* (London: Withers).

HARRIS, W. T. (1887) Editor's Preface to Froebel's *Education of Man*, trans. Hailmann (Concord, Mass.).

HARTUNG, C. V. (1956) 'Doctrines of English Usage' (*English Journal*, XLV, December. Reprinted in Dean and Wilson, 1959).

HILL, A. A. (1954) 'Prescriptivism and Linguistics in English Teaching' (*College English*, April 1954. Reprinted in Allen, 1958).

HORNBY, A. S. (1954) *A Guide to Pattern and Usage in English* (London: O.U.P.).

HOTOPF, W. H. N. (1965) *Language, Thought and Comprehension* (London: Routledge and Kegan Paul).

JESPERSEN, O. (1925) *Mankind, Nation and Individual from a Linguistic Point of View* (Oslo: Aschehoug); 1909–49. *A Modern English Grammar* (seven volumes) (Heidelberg, Copenhagen, London: Allen & Unwin).

JOOS, M. (1962) *The Five Clocks* (Indiana University and Mouton).

KEATINGE, M. W. (1896) *Introduction to translation of Comenius: The Great Didactic* (London: Black).

KENNEDY, A. G. (1942) *English Usage: A Study in Policy and Procedure* (N.C.T.E. Monograph No. 15) (New York: Appleton-Century).

KNOWLES, J. (1785) 4th edition 1796 *Principles of English Grammar* (Liverpool: Hodgson).

KRAPP, G. P. (1927) *A Comprehensive Guide to Good English* (New York: Rand McNally).

LANDOR, W. S. (1824–29) *Imaginary Conversations of Literary Men and Statesmen* (London: Taylor and Hessey).

LEACOCK, S. (1944) *How to Write* (London: Bodley Head).

LEONARD, S. A. (1929) *The Doctrine of Correctness in English Usage, 1700-1800* (University of Wisconsin Studies in Language and Literature, No. 25, Madison); (1932) *Current English Usage* (Chicago: N.C.T.E.).

LEWIS, N. (1949) 'How Correct Must English Be?' *Harper's Magazine*, Vol. 198, No. 1186, pp. 68–74 (New York).

LIEBERMAN, L. (1964) *Correct English Usage* (London: Peter Owen).

LOUNSBURY, T. R. (1908) *The Standard of Usage in English* (New York: Harper).

LOW, W. H., & HOLLINGWORTH, G. E. (1941) (3rd edition) *Matriculation English Course* (London: University Tutorial Press).

LOWTH, R. (1762) *A Short Introduction to English Grammar* (London: J. Hughs).

LYMAN, R. L. (1929) *Summary of Investigations relating to Grammar, Language and Composition* (Illinois: University of Chicago).

MACDONALD, DWIGHT (1962) 'The String Untuned' (New Yorker. Reprinted in Dean and Wilson, 1959).

MARCKWARDT, A. H., & WALCOTT, F. (1938) *Facts about Current English Usage* (New York: Appleton-Century).

MASON, G. (1622) *Grammaire Anglaise* (London: Butter).

MATTHEWS, BRANDER (1901) *Parts of Speech—Essays on English* (New York: Scribner).

MOORE, G. (1959) 'American Prose Today' (New World Writing, No. 8. Reprinted in Dean and Wilson, 1959).

MURRAY, LINDLEY (1795) *English Grammar, adapted to the different classes of learners* (York: Wilson Spence and Mawman).

PARTRIDGE, E. (1947) *Usage and Abusage* (London: Hamish Hamilton).

PERRIN, P. G. (1939) *An Index to English: Handbook of Current Usage and Style* (New York: Scott).

POOLEY, R. C. (1946) *Teaching English Usage:* N.C.T.E. Monograph No. 16 (New York: Appleton-Century); (1960) 'Dare Schools Set a Standard in English Usage?' (*English Journal*, XLIX, March. Reprinted in Dean and Wilson, 1959).

POTTER, S. (1950) *Our Language* (London: Penguin).

PRIESTLEY, J. (1761) *The Rudiments of English Grammar* (London: Griffiths).

QUIRK, R. (1960) *The Use of English* (London: Longmans).

QUIRK, R., & SVARTVIK, J. (1966) *Investigating Linguistic Acceptability* (Hague: Mouton. Janua Linguarum, Series Minor No. LIV).

RICHARDS, I. A. (1955) *Speculative Instruments* (London: Routledge and Kegan Paul).

SAPIR, E. (1921) *Language* (New York: Harcourt, Brace).

SCHLAUCH, M. (1959) (reprinted 1967) *The English Language in Modern Times* (London: O.U.P.)

SLEDD, JAMES (1962) 'The Lexicographer's Uneasy Chair' (*College English* XXIII, May 1962. Reprinted in Dean and Wilson, 1959).

SMITH, LOGAN PEARSALL (1925) *Words and Idioms* (London: Constable).

STORY, JOSHUA (1778) 3rd edition 1783 *An Introduction to English Grammar* (Newcastle).

STRANG, BARBARA M. H. (1962) *Modern English Structure* (London: Edward Arnold).

SWEET, H. (1876) 'Words, Logic and Grammar'. Collected Papers of Henry Sweet, arr. H. C. Wyld (Oxford, 1913).

TREBLE, H. A., & VALLINS, G. H. (1936) *A B C of English Usage* (Oxford: Clarendon Press).

VALLINS, G. H. (1951) *Good English: How to Write It.* (London: Pan Books); (1953) *Better English* (London: Pan Books).

WALLIS, J. (1653) *Grammatica Linguæ Anglicanæ* (Oxford).

WARD, W. (1765?) *An Essay on Grammar, as it may be applied to the English Language* (London: Horsfield).

WEBSTER, N. (1789) *Dissertations on the English Language* (Boston); (1920) *Webster's New International Dictionary*, revised.

WEST, M., & KIMBER, P. F. (1957) *Deskbook of Current English* (London: Longmans).

WHITE, RICHARD GRANT (1870) revised 1899 *Words and Their Uses, Past and Present: A Study of the English Language* (New York: Houghton, Mifflin).

WHITTEN, W., & WHITAKER, F. (1939) *Good and Bad English* (London: Newnes)

WILKINSON, A. *et al.* (1965) *Spoken English* (University of Birmingham).